THE UNIVERSITY OF MICHIGAN
CENTER FOR CHINESE STUDIES


MICHIGAN ABSTRACTS OF CHINESE AND
JAPANESE WORKS ON CHINESE HISTORY
NO. 6

T0349895

*THE PAWNSHOP IN CHINA*

by T. S. Whelan

Based on Yang Chao-yü, *Chung-kuo tien-tang yeh*
[The Chinese pawnbroking industry], with a historical introduction and critical annotations.

Ann Arbor

Center for Chinese Studies
The University of Michigan

1979

Originally published in Chinese as

Yang Chao-yü, *Chung-kuo tien-tang yeh*
[The Chinese Pawnbroking Industry]

中國典當業

(Shanghai: The Commercial Press Ltd., 1929)

Printed in the United States of America

Cover woodcut is from *Lu Hsün Hua Chuan*
魯迅畫傳 [A pictorial biography of
Lu Hsün] (Hong Kong: Sun Chau Book
Company 神州圖書公司, 1975), p. 59.
Entitled "Pawnshop and Pharmacy," the
woodcut shows Lu Hsün as a youth
leaving a pawnshop.

For Professor Chou Hung-hsiang,
who first brought the matter
of Chinese pawnbroking to the
writer's attention.

# CONTENTS

Part One

    Antecedents                                                 1

Part Two

    The Pawnshop in Late Imperial and
    Republican Times                17

        The Large Chinese Pawnshop, 1875 to 1928

            Exteriors, Interiors and Fixtures      21

            Additional Comments on *Tien, Tang, Chih,*
                *Ya* and *Tai-tang*           24

            *Tien* and *Tang* Pawnshop Organization   25

            Business            31

            Management         38

            Pawn Tickets and Ledgers     42

            Wages, Dividends and Commissions   46

            Taxation of Pawnshops     50

            Pawn Ticket Handwriting Style and
                Terminology         50

Notes                                        53

Glossary                               71

Bibliography                        79

PART ONE

ANTECEDENTS AND HISTORY

The pawnshop in China dates from the last quarter of the fifth century A.D. The Japanese scholar Abe Takeo traces its origins rather precisely to the Southern Ch'i dynasty (A.D. 479-502).[1] At that time the Chinese pawnshop was a commercial enterprise restricted to Buddhist monasteries, wherein it was to remain for several hundred years. From the T'ang onward to the end of the Yüan, however, this oldest of all Chinese credit institutions extended beyond temple precincts to the laity, so that monks and laymen concurrently acted as pawnbrokers. As an illustration of the derivative nature of the newer lay pawnshops, Miyazaki Michisaburō notes that during the Sung, lay proprietors wore black gowns in imitation of the black robes of Buddhist monks.[2] Under the Ming dynasty the temple pawnshop gradually disappeared, and the business thereafter became the province of the laity.

The Ch'ing dynasty witnessed a phenomenal rise in the number of pawnshops. By the early nineteenth century there were almost 25,000 of them, and pawnbroking yielded a higher rate of return on investment than did land. The Ch'ing also saw this industry in decline, its exponential growth a victim of the Taiping Rebellion and rapidly developing Shansi banks. Yet, in republican times the pawnshop was still common in city and countryside alike. Furthermore, it was to live on after Liberation. But when the People's Bank of China opened Citizens' Petty Loan Offices in the early 1950s in order to furnish workers and peasants with low-interest loans, and when the transformation of private enterprise occurred in 1956, the last of the pawnbrokers, holding out in urban areas such as Shanghai, were forced to close their doors, and the pawnshop ceased to exist on the mainland.[3] Its life had spanned almost fifteen hundred years. On Taiwan, however, the institution survives--there were 750 pawnshops on the island in 1974--as it does in most overseas Chinese communities.

There can be little doubt that the pawnshop flourished in Chinese Buddhist communities during the period of political disunion known as the Six Dynasties. Documents found at Tunhuang and elsewhere also suggest that this historical era marked the earliest appearance of pawnbroking in China. Abe Takeo does not stand alone with this thesis; there is a large body of informed opinion--Chinese, Japanese and Western--in agreement with him. On the other hand, two Chinese scholars, Mi Kung-kan and Yang Chao-yü, who have written extensively on the pawnshop in

1

China, attempt to trace its origins to the later Han.[4,5] They both cite a passage from the biography of Liu Yü in the *History of the Later Han:*

後漢書劉虞傳:「虞所資賞,典當胡夷,瓚數抄奪之.」

which on the surface might be translated:

> What was bestowed [by the state] upon [Liu] Yü was pawned by him to a Tartar. [The Duke's grandson] Tsuan made several attempts to get it back by force.[6]

As evidence of pawnbroking in China prior to the fifth century A.D., this quotation would appear to be a hapax legomenon. Nothing further has been produced from the written record in support of Mi's and Yang's contention that the practice dates from Later Han times (circa A.D. 100-200). The term *tien-tang,* meaning "to pawn," is also a fairly recent one, not in general use until the Ch'ing dynasty. Furthermore, the action of Tsuan, the third party in the passage, is suspect. Forcibly intervening to repossess a pawned article certainly does not fall within the usual pattern of a pawning transaction, that is, of redeeming a chattel through some form of payment, normally by the person making the pledge. Finally, Lien-sheng Yang concludes that *tien-tang* here suggests the giving of tribute: "Although it is known that foreign merchants from the northwest were active in China under the Han dynasty, it is doubtful whether the expression . . . means pawnbroking as in comparatively modern usage, because the passage certainly refers to gifts made by [Liu] Yü to barbarians in order to appease them."[7]

Having fixed pawnbroking in China as a monastic enterprise in the period of political disunion in the fifth century, but not earlier, it remains to be asked whether the practice was sui generis or the result of cultural diffusion. Once again, the historical record is exiguous, and the opinions of noted scholars of Buddhism differ.

Kenneth Chen believes that the pawnshop was unknown to the sanghas of India and suggests that when the institution did appear in China, it was in consequence of the interaction between Buddhism, newly arrived on the scene, and the rather advanced Chinese money economy which obtained at the time. Chen argues that the temple pawnshop, to which surplus funds from the "inexhaustible treasury" (*wu-chin tsang*) were channeled, was a manifestation of the sinification of Buddhism.[8] Whether the use made

of them was for profit or for public welfare is another issue and
will be discussed below.

Jacques Gernet, however, thinks it is possible that India
introduced pawnbroking to China via Buddhist communities in Central Asia, and that as far as China was concerned, it was an entirely
new concept in the borrowing and lending of money. He implies
then that the pawnshop might have been a part of Buddhist financial life in India earlier on.[9]

In China, pawnbroking was probably a lineal descendant of
the ancient custom of exchanging political hostages (*chiao-chih*)
between neighboring or contending states. These hostages
frequently were members of the aristocracy or even of the ruling
house:

趙太后新用事，秦急攻之，趙氏求救
於齊，齊曰：「必以長安君為質，兵乃出」
太后不肯，大臣強諫。太后明謂左右：「有
復言令長安君為質者，老婦必唾其面」

No sooner had the Empress Dowager of Chao taken
power than the State of Ch'in launched an attack.
Whereupon Chao appealed for help from the State
of Ch'i. Ch'i responded: "We will dispatch troops
when you send the Prince of Ch'ang An to us as a
hostage." But the Empress Dowager refused. And
when her ministers went to great lengths to warn
her of the consequences, she answered them in no
uncertain terms: "If anyone dares to speak of this
matter again, I shall spit in his face."[10]

The character *chih*, 質 , which is here used for "a hostage,"
came to mean "an earnest" or "a pledge" and subsequently became
a general term for the Buddhist institutiton of pawning during the
Six Dynasties and the T'ang.[11] *Chih-k'u* referred to the temple
pawnshop itself, while *chih-chü* came to mean "pawn loans"; and
when in the late T'ang money became the sole means of redemption
in pawning transactions (rather than goods or grain), such money
was called *chih-ch'ien*. It was at this time too (the Kamakura period)
that the pawnshop was introduced by Buddhist monks into Japan.[12]
To the present day the Japanese equivalent of the Chinese col-
loquial *tang-p'u* is *shichiya*, (i.e., *chih-wu*).

If pawnbroking in the Chinese experience descended directly from the practice of exchanging political hostages, a relationship which is rather obscure, it should come as no surprise whatsoever that the Chinese pawnbroker was a nephew of the Chinese moneylender.[13] Moneylending, which seems to predate pawnbroking wherever in the world the latter occurs, appeared in China as early as the fourth century B.C.[14] By the Han dynasty, moneylenders were known as "interest-making specialists" (tzu-ch'ien chia).[15]

In sum, Chinese pawnbroking derived from practices that had harsh consequences; for bondage was an ingredient in the lives of both the hostage from the ruling class and the hapless peasant borrower, to whom default on a debt to a moneylender could mean years of servitude or permanent enslavement. Pawnbroking was innovative in part because it no longer subjected a borrower to this bondage in the case of nonpayment, but only caused him to forfeit the chattel in pawn, even though this might be a vital one such as his padded winter jacket or plough. Clearly, to repeat Gernet's phrase, pawnbroking was a "new concept in the borrowing and lending of money."[16,17]

What then of the economic climate by the time of the Six Dynasties when this credit institution was born? The economic antecedents of the pawnshop had long been in existence. Trade, for example, had been conducted for several thousand years on the North China Plain. With it went various media of exchange, from cowrie shells in ancient times, through bronze "spade" and "knife" money by the third century B.C., to silks and coins. But the prerequisite that made moneylending, and hence pawnbroking, possible was the concentrated accumulation of surplus capital hand in hand with a widespread scarcity of cash. Paul Wheatley remarks that as early as the Chan-kuo period there had already been a progression in China "from a familial lord-and-subject bond, through the contractual lien of creditor and debtor, to the impersonal relationship of master and hired hand."[18] Naturally it was the master who put his surplus capital to work in lending it out at (often usurious rates of) interest, and it was the hired hand whose abject condition forced him to borrow, often merely to survive.[19]

Turning now to the Buddhist temples whose monks were the first pawnbrokers, we see once again this phenonemon of surplus capital accumulation. Kenneth Chen writes that "the economy of the Buddhist monastic community was based on the idea of exchange. The faithful layman donated alms to the clerical order or material goods to the monastery. In return the sangha made a gift of the law to the layman. Both parties were happy and satisfied with this exchange. If such goods as were presented to the sangha were not excessive and could be easily consumed, the problem of surplus did not arise. But it often happened that the contributions of the laity exceeded the needs of the sangha. To take care of this surplus, and to dispose of it, an institution known as the inexhaustible treasury was established in the temple."[20] In addition to the alms of the faithful, the monastery took in revenues from estates, "donated in the main by members of the imperial household, the nobility, and the great families of the realm."[21] These monies, too, accrued to the inexhaustible treasury.

The funds in this treasury were given by people from all walks of life who desired temple monks to offer prayers on their behalf to their ancestors. These funds were therefore originally called "ancestral temple silver" (tz'u-t'ang yin). Subsequently, they were known both as "long life cash" (ch'ang-sheng ch'ien) and "inexhaustible resources" (wu-chin ts'ai), from which came the term "inexhaustible treasury." (An early name for treasury funds earmarked for temple pawnshop use was "long life treasury" [ch'ang sheng k'u], which was derived from the first of these terms.)[22]

In the sphere of general economic activity, the Chinese Buddhist monastery in the fifth century (like the Christian monastery of Europe during the Middle Ages) established inns for the traveler and public baths, cared for the sick and buried the dead, operated water mills and oil presses, and, finally, loaned money and stored other people's valuables, twin concerns of subsequent lay pawnshops.[23]

There is no doubt that by late T'ang times temple pawnshops charged high rates of interest on loans to peasants. Chen observes that "for the year 924 the Ching-t'u Temple in Tunhuang noted that out of a total of 366.9 shih of grain received by the granary, only 44.4 shih or 12 percent represented revenue from the temple lands; more than 200 shih or 55 percent were taken in as interest, and the rest, 120 shih or 33 percent, constituted donations."[24] It is not clear, however, whether or not the original intent of pawnbroker monks in the Six Dynasties was to lend money at interest. Once more, expert opinion is divided, this time over the issue of "for profit or for social welfare." Abe Takeo states that in the first instance the purpose of the monastic pawnshop was the public welfare (kung-i).[25] Niida Noboru corroborates Abe's remark; temple pawnshops originally loaned to the poor for the benefit of the poor. It was as an act of social welfare and not designed to fill the treasury coffers by charging interest.[26]

Indeed, Niida continues, Stein and Pelliot found early pawn contract forms (wen-shu, literally "documents") at Tunhuang on which there was "no column for the obligation of payment of interest." On one such form found by Stein, "a monk in a Buddhist temple in A.D. 782 loaned seven *p'i* of silk, two and a half *p'i* to be returned within a year, the remaining four and a half *p'i* within five years." Another form discovered by Stein, also dated A.D. 782, pertained to a certain person named Huo Hsin-yüeh, who borrowed a "weight of chestnuts" from a pawnbroker monk and promised to return it in the September of the same year. (Presumably this meant an equal weight of new chestnuts gathered at harvest time.) In this case, however, the form specified that if Huo Hsin-yüeh defaulted, his personal property to the value of the chestnuts would be seized, as well as a further amount for penalty. But even here, there is nothing at all concerning interest, as such. Niida comments that originally, monks loaned not only chestnuts and silk but also wheat and money to peasants at no interest; and that when a commodity was borrowed in the pawning transaction, the same commodity was returned, except in the case of money, where wheat or rice instead could on occasion be used to repay the value of the loan. Once again, there is no mention of interest.[27] Finally, Niida relates that in the earliest text to explain pawnbroking, the Yüan "Civil Servants' Manual" (*Li-hsüeh chih-nan*), there is a section dealing with pawning contracts in which "loans without interest" are discussed.[28] In sum, both Abe and Niida agree that monastic pawnbroking was originally interest-free in China, and that only after the decline in prestige of the Buddhist temples during the T'ang dynasty did monks frequently become in effect usurers, or in Niida's phrase, "selfish loaners."[29]

Chen, on the other hand, qualifies the remarks of Abe and Niida. It was only those peasants "attached to the monastery . . . [who] enjoyed special treatment and were permitted to borrow grain without any payment of interest." In Chen's opinion, all other pawn loans were at interest. (He is speaking of Tunhuang, a region, he says, which although remote, mirrored the economic activities of Buddhist temples elsewhere in China.) Among these, he differentiates loans to privileged families for the long-term and "usually in money or fabrics' and the short-term loans in grain to "peasants not connected to the monastery" at high rates of interest.[30]

By the T'ang-Sung period, pawning at interest was the order of the day, both for temple and lay pawnshops, including those lay pawnshops that were established in temples to avoid taxation. Most temples enjoyed a tax-exempt status, and this exemption applied to any business enterprise conducted within their precincts. It should be pointed out, however, that not all Buddhist sects practiced pawnbroking.

Other features of the pawning procedure can also be observed at this time. Collateral now had to be provided in the form of a chattel. In the T'ang dynasty, the character *tien* ("to mortgage") was used for the item held as collateral, whether it was a precious object from a well-to-do family or a peasant's farm implement; later *tien* denoted a particular category of pawnshop (as described in Part Two below). The borrower also had to find other persons to stand as his guarantors (called *fang-shou jen*) and sometimes find special guarantees (*pao-cheng*) as well. Contracts were now called *chüan-ch'i* and *ch'i-cheng*; these were the forerunners of the pawn ticket and the stipulations thereon. Witnesses to the pawning transaction itself were also occasionally required. It would appear that originally the above precautions were not deemed necessary, for Lien-sheng Yang writes that certain inexhaustible treasury funds (that is to say, *ch'ang-sheng k'u*) were loaned without any guarantees whatever on the grounds that "most borrowers [would] pay back . . . for fear of divine retribution."[31]

Before discussing the directions that pawnbroking was to take, we might first stop and consider the question: was there a conflict of spiritual and temporal interests when Chinese Buddhist monks turned to profit-making activities, such as pawnbroking, and when they became essentially usurers?[32] No, says Chen: "Strange as it may seem the Buddhist canon in China specifically provided that if goods donated to the temples were not entirely utilized by the monks or nuns, such surplus goods could be sold or loaned out and the profits used to defray expenses incurred in repairing temples or stupas."[33]

Yet, the monasteries' money-raising activities and the resulting wealth which accumulated in their inexhaustible treasuries contributed to the Hui-Ch'ang suppression of A.D. 845. Niida claims that many monks profited outrageously from pawnbroking and that prior to the suppression, the institution had spread to the poorer temples (among those sects that engaged in it). Great numbers of peasants suffered at the hands of these monks through high-interest pawn loans, often caught in the vicious circle of borrowing a second time to meet the principal and interest of an initial loan, a third time to pay off a second, and so on.[34] Even so, by the terms of the act of grace decreed by Emperor Wu-tsung following the Hui-Ch'ang suppression, the Buddhist temples were granted permission to reengage in all their commerical activities and reestablish their inexhaustible treasuries.

Of course, Buddhist monks were not the only "selfish loaners" in the T'ang-Sung period. High interest rates prevailed in the lay pawnshops owned by court officials (usually through intermediaries), landed gentry, and rich merchants.[35] Thus pawnbroking, which probably began its life in the period of political disunion as an instrument of social welfare, had now become, according to Abe, the "most stable and safe" of businesses among both monks and laity. Peasants accepted high interest rates in pawning as a matter of course.[36] It was, after all, the least painful way of obtaining ready cash or vital grains and other commodities.[37]

Also during the T'ang-Sung period, the names by which pawnshops were known became more differentiated. *Chi-fu p'u* was a common term for a lay pawnshop under the T'ang, while *chih-k'u*--originally the temple pawnshop in the Six Dynasties--and *chieh-k'u* were widespread names for the same type of shop under the Sung.[38] From the twelfth century on, the term *ch'ang-sheng k'u*, once applied only to special treasury funds in the monasteries set aside for use in their pawnbroking activities, was given to all temple pawnshops.[39] (Beginning in the Ming dynasty, *ch'ang-sheng k'u* became the literary expression for a pawnshop.)[40]

In the Sung, the *ch'ang-sheng k'u* were also known inside Taoist temples. Hino Kaizaburō reports that Buddhist monks and Taoist priests used these temple pawnshop profits to pay the government for ordination licenses (called *tu-tieh*) with which they obtained the rank of monk or priest. Such licenses were both obligatory and very expensive, and large amounts of capital were needed to acquire them. During this time, the *ch'ang-sheng k'u* also accepted funds on deposit from wealthy laymen, thus functioning as a kind of savings bank. These deposits were considered desirable because they were safe, accumulated interest, and money could easily be withdrawn from them.[41]

The government-operated or "official" pawnshop (*ti-tang k'u*) made its first appearance in the Southern Sung dynasty. This new establishment used its profits mainly to meet military expenditures and should be distinguished from certain later private (lay) pawnshops in which government at the district level often invested (to be discussed in Part Two). The Southern Sung was also noted for the increased power and scope of its lay pawnshops, especially in such southeastern cities as Hangchow, where the hold of Buddhism was relatively weak. In order for the rich to maintain their luxurious lifestyles in the face of inflation brought on by the Mongol invasions to the north, they were forced to increase their incomes. Many turned to pawnbroking, and in 1275 there were dozens of pawnshops in Hangchow alone.[42] Despite the weakness of the Buddhist temples in that city--or perhaps because of it--wealthy businessmen, relatives of the Court, eunuchs, and others opened pawnshops inside them to take advantage of their exemption from the property tax (*shui-mai*) charged outside.

Miyazaki mentions a certain method of investment undertaken at this time: the pooling of capital in a "pawning partnership," known as a *chü*. Ten well-to-do men invested equal amounts of money for equal shares. At the close of each year for the next ten years, one of the ten men only--in accordance with a prearranged roster--withdrew the total profits of the *chü* for that year while leaving his capital untouched. At the expiration of the ten year period, the pool was dissolved and each man then reclaimed his original capital outlay.[43]

Even though the monastic pawnshop continued in operation throughout the Yüan dynasty well into the fourteenth century, benefiting from imperial decrees that exempted it from taxation, the lay pawnshop became more and more dominant. Under Mongol rule, it was called *chieh-tien k'u*.[44] According to Lien-sheng Yang, "the term . . . was so popular that its transliteration is found in Mongolian texts of Yüan decrees."[45] After the Yüan, the temple shop disappeared, and, as Yang also remarks, the lay pawnshop "developed so much [in the Ming] that most people forgot that the institution was once confined to monasteries. One or more pawnshops would be found in every city and town and in many villages."[46]

Except for the disappearance of the temple pawnshop and the issue by the government of detailed regulations regarding lay pawnshops' interest rates and pledge periods (which apparently met with a high degree of compliance), the Ming and early Ch'ing periods witnessed no significant changes regarding pawnbroking, though the terms *tien-tang* and *tang-p'u* for "pawnshop" came into wide use. Soon, however, several major developments were to alter the picture drastically and cause pawnbroking by the reign of the Ch'ien-lung Emperor (1736-1796) to reach a level of prosperity it had never known and one it would enjoy until the beginning of the Kuang-hsü reign (1875). These developments were a change in the rural ("manorial") order, the abolition of the poll-tax (*ting-fu*), a decline in the number of salt merchants, and the large-scale entrusting of public monies to pawnbrokers for purposes of investment.

Of the countryside in the eighteenth century, Mark Elvin comments that "serfdom . . . finally disappeared, and a new . . . rural order took shape. The landlord and the pawnbroker took the place of the manorial lord; financial relationships displaced those of status. The . . . gentry who ran rural projects now did so as professional managers. . . ."[47] A consequence of this collapse of the old manorial order was that peasants, caught in the grip of seasonal shortages, could no longer turn to the manorial organization to tide them over, but in ever increasing numbers were forced to turn to the pawnbroker instead. It was said that a poor tenant " 'would rather default on [his] rent than dare not to pay back [his] debt to the grain-lender [i.e., the pawnbroker], for fear that in the latter case [he] might be unable to borrow again the following year.' " It was also said that " 'these days the activities of rich persons in agriculture consist in the exercise of skill in lending money at interest.' Financial resources were thus in many ways becoming a more important source of social and economic power in the countryside than ownership of land."[48]

Yet, during the eighteenth century the "people flourished," in Abe's phrase, in the sense that "the work force became enormous and the economy proceeded at full throttle." Although a contributing factor to this prosperity was no doubt the long period of peace in the empire, its prime cause was most likely the abolition of the poll-tax during the K'ang-hsi reign (1662-1723) in favor of a tax system much reduced in severity.[49] For it was not long after this relaxation of fiscal pressure that the economic boom manifested itself.

Pawnbroking kept abreast of the times. While there were 9,904 pawnshops in 1723, there were some 19,000 by mid-century, and by the early 1800s probably 25,000 of them.[50] Where did all these pawnbrokers come from? This question can be answered in part by noting another major development: the tapering off of the salt trade, heretofore the largest in China and one which had attracted much of her investment capital. Its decline in the eighteenth century caused the salt merchants to defect in droves and invest heavily in pawnbroking, which was increasingly considered as safer and more profitable. This shift turned the tables and now made pawnbroking China's biggest business.[51]

The last of the important eighteenth-century developments that shaped the pawnbroking industry was the handing over of public funds to pawnbrokers (and other businessmen) for investing (fa-shang sheng-hsi, "entrusting to merchants to produce profit"). This widespread practice was doubtless welcomed by private investors in pawnshops since it tended to minimize their risk. Interest charged by the government was on the order of 2 percent per month. (Pawnbrokers naturally passed this charge on to borrowers, together with an additional 1 percent per month, which was understood to constitute a "commission." Borrowers therefore paid on average 3 percent per month, or 36 percent per year, in interest on loans.[52]) The state utilized this interest earned on its funds in many ways: for famine relief and the upkeep of impoverished bannermen, for student scholarships, the running of orphanages, and the like.[53]

As pawnbroking became safe and profitable in the eighteenth century, the social status of the pawnbroker increased. Indeed, he enjoyed more prestige than in any previous dynasty.[54]

The pawnshops themselves were "required to register with the government and to pay a license fee or tax."[55] Abe Takeo probably refers in part to these regulations when he speaks of the "development in quality" of the Ch'ing pawnshops. Since they were under tighter government control than before, management had to be more accountable in consequence. He also refers to the variety of pawnshops available to the borrowing public (the tien and tang, and the smaller chih and ya, detailed below in Part Two)[56] and to regional variants, such as the an-type shops to be found in Fukien and Kwangtung.[57]

One common eighteenth-century pawning practice should be noted before progressing to late Ch'ing and early republican times: *t'un-tang* "pawn hoarding," or pawning for speculation. According to Lien-sheng Yang, "certain hoarders [in grains] even utilized loans thus acquired to double or redouble their speculation. For instance, with 1000 taels of silver, one could purchase a number of bushels of rice. Pawning the rice for seven or eight hundred taels, one could use the sum to purchase more rice. This process might be repeated four or five times. As a result, one could hoard rice worth four or five thousand taels with his original capital of one thousand taels. This would yield a considerable profit, especially when there was an understanding between the hoarder and the pawnbroker and when the interest rate charged by the latter was relatively low. . . . To stop such hoarding for speculation, the government limited loans based on grain security to small amounts."[58]

Abe notes a decline in pawnbroking during the course of the Kuang-hsü reign and a "heavy falloff" thereafter.[59] Two principal reasons are usually cited for this development: one economic and the other political. The former affected the larger, more heavily capitalized *tien* and *tang* pawnshops in the cities; the latter took its toll on the smaller *chih* and *ya* pawnshops in the countryside.[60] Statistics bear witness to the results. Whereas in 1800 there were twenty-five thousand pawnshops, by the 1930s there were only forty-five hundred of them.[61]

The first reason for the decline was that the pawnbroking industry in late imperial times suffered from the competition of the traditional as well as modern banks in the area of loan making. Shansi banks, for example, not only charged extremely low rates of interest on loans but only on rare occasions required collateral from those of their preferred customers who wished to secure them. These customers had hitherto formed the nucleus of the urban clientèle, patronizing the large, publicly funded *tien* (*kung-chi tien*) and privately financed *tang* pawnshops both as pawners and depositors.[62] Despite the fact that these shops cut their interest rates (and the government in the nineteenth century lowered its interest rate on public funds invested in *tien* shops from 1 to 2 percent), they simply could not compete with the Shansi banks. Nor could they compete with other traditional or modern banks, both of whose rates--although slightly higher than the Shansi banks-- were still well below those of the large pawnshops.[63] (The *chih* and *ya* shops typically charged higher interest over a shorter pledge period than did the *tien* and *tang* shops, dealt with a far poorer clientèle, and mainly loaned small sums of money on pledges of low value, such as farm implements, utensils and homespun cloth.)

As a result, the publicly funded *tien* shops rapidly disappeared as the government ceased investing in pawnbroking. Iseki Takao reports that at the end of the Ch'ing dynasty they could be found only in Nanking. During the early years of the republic, then, with their public funds withdrawn, *tien* shops became strictly privately owned establishments and tended to merge with *tang* shops in the public mind. Such was the legacy of government funding, however, that these shops were known as *kung-tien* and *kung-tang*, that is, they were not considered to be set up for private profit, erroneous as this notion was. There is no doubt as to the "private" nature of the smaller shops, and they were called *szu-chih* and *szu-ya*, and in Fukien and Kwangtung, *szu-an*.[64]

Pawnbroking also suffered from the unsettled political conditions that followed in the wake of the Taiping Rebellion, particularly in the countryside. Frequent inflation and regional currency devaluation caused the wholesale closing down of rural pawnshops. Peasants would speedily redeem articles with depreciated currency, which would wipe out pawnshops overnight. (These business failures were known as "closed-down pawnshops" [*hsieh-yeh tien-tien*].) Accordingly, such capital as was now invested in this shrinking industry was concentrated in Shanghai, Peking, Nanking, Tientsin, Hankow, Canton, Tsingtao and other cities. The pawnshops in these centers numbered about one thousand, or a quarter of all Chinese shops. If other cities and large towns linked by rail are taken into consideration, then urban pawnshops accounted for over half of the total.[65]

The exodus of pawnbroking from the countryside was remedied early in the republic by a unique institution termed a "pawnbroking agency" (*tai-tang* or *tai-pu*). So important were these *tai-tang*, remarks Iseki, that pawnbroking in this period cannot be discussed without giving them serious consideration.[66] Essentially, they were small rural agencies representing large, city-based pawnshops. As such, they performed two key functions: providing a substitute service in the absence of the regular pawnshops; and later, after the restoration of law and order, acting as the vanguard for the pawnshops' return.

Located in a village or a market town, a *tai-tang* received operating funds from a particular urban pawnshop and either forwarded items in pledge to it (for reasons of safekeeping or lack of storage facilities) or kept them and "carried on business under the supervision of [its] principals."[67] If such a *tai-tang* forwarded a pawned article to its parent city shop, it charged the borrower a handling fee (*shou-shu liao*) of 5 percent.[68] Due to the rural unrest in the midst of which it operated and the absence of government controls or scrutiny, a *tai-tang* usually charged the borrower very high rates of interest over short periods of redemption. A *tai-tang* was also only rarely subject to taxation; and when it was, the tax was apt to be light, far less than that paid by the urban pawnshop during the same time.[69]

Iseki believes there is evidence to suggest that after more settled conditions returned to the countryside and "law and order gradually expanded [under Kuomintang rule],"[70] the *tai-tang* "also expanded in the rural areas."[71] This statement, however, must be taken with a grain of salt because there was now a movement of the large *tien* and *tang* pawnshops back to the villages and market towns where the *tai-tang* that had been there before were fulfilling the role of vanguard. Many of these *tien* and *tang* shops tried to pass as *tai-tang* in order to circumvent the taxation and interest restrictions imposed on them in the cities. Rural *tai-tang* expansion is therefore open to serious question.[72]

As indicated earlier, pawnbroking during the republican period reverted almost entirely to private entrepreneurs, public funding having been withdrawn as the business became something of an investment risk. The result was that the overwhelming majority of pawnshops at this time were owned either jointly by wealthy families or outright by a single family. Frequently a single family owned many shops of different categories; that is, *tien, tang, chih,* or *ya.* The government-run pawnshop--never an important part of the Chinese pawnbroking equation--and the pawnshop in the hands of other public bodies were exceptions to the rule (though in contrast, as will be shown below, government-run pawnshops are very much in evidence today on Taiwan).[73]

Now that pawnbroking had returned to the countryside, 3,386 of China's 4,500 pawnshops (that is, about 75 percent) in operation on the eve of Japanese aggression were rural. Most borrowers then were peasants, with urban factory workers also accounting for a substantial number. It is therefore not surprising that the value of most pawn tickets was very low.[74] During the 1930s in a village near Peking, for example, 90 percent of the pawn tickets had a value of three dollars or less, and of these, one-third were worth only fifty cents.[75] R. H. Tawney notes, however, that peasants at this same time, apart from small loans for consumption expenditures, also used rural pawnshops for large loans to meet "crisis" expenses, such as weddings and funerals.[76]

During the republican period, there was also a trend towards increasingly shorter periods of redemption offered by pawnshops. This trend developed for two reasons: as a hedge against inflation, currency devaluation, and the withdrawal of certain coinage from circulation; and because of fast and frequent changes in clothing fashions.[77]

It would appear that pawnbroking in China under the Japanese occupation continued at the level of operation it had reached in 1930, that is, at approximately forty-five hundred pawnshops. It is reported, however, that the Japanese made a practice of removing Chinese managerial personnel and substituting Koreans, doubtless for the purpose of tighter surveillance.[78] It is of special interest that during the occupation itself many Japanese economists wrote and published works on Chinese pawnbroking. Niida's and Iseki's papers, cited above, appeared in 1937 and 1941, respectively. Hayashi Kōhei, who wrote on the contemporary pawnshop in Nanking, Hangchow and Wusih, published his findings in 1943.[79]

As noted earlier, pawnbroking lingered on after Liberation but disappeared by the mid-1950s after the transformation of private enterprise effected in 1956. But the industry's demise was foreshadowed--if not by the tenets of socialism itself--by at least three prior developments. The first was the establishment in 1953 of Citizens' Petty Loan Offices of the People's Bank of China and has already been mentioned. If the chief aim of these offices was to provide petty loans at low cost, then their secondary objective was to break the back "of the established pawnbroking business" by doing so.[80]

The second development was the formation of the rural loan system, a "radical departure from past practice" in that it was not only "a simple monetary measure" but also an instrument of state policy. That is to say, it granted loans almost exclusively to mutual-aid teams ("organized" laboring farmers) and only rarely to individuals.[81] Thus, rural finance was taken out of the hands of any landlords (often in the guise of pawnbrokers) who might still remain.

The last development concerned itself with the countryside after those landlords had become dispossessed under land reform. This was the setting up of credit cooperatives, which successfully filled "the vacuum left by the collapse of [these] private sources of credit." In the early years of the program, however, it appears that there was residual usury and pawnbroking, due to spot shortages of "short-term capital in agriculture and a lack of banking facilities in remote areas."[82]

Taiwan, of course, presents a totally different picture. The pawnbroking industry on the island, far from disappearing, seems to have enjoyed a steady growth, despite some reverses. While at the end of the Japanese occupation there were approximately 50 pawnshops, in 1974, as mentioned above, there were 750. Most of these were in private hands, but some were run by municipal authorities which had entered pawnbroking during the 1950s in order "to gain a share of the profits and to exert more control over the

business."[83]  This was a period of scarcity, and private pawnbroking returned an enormous profit, with the shops frequently charging 25 percent interest per month.  By intervening and charging
far lower interest rates, local governments checked these usurious
terms on which money was being made available to the poor, thus
affording them some relief.  It also made it more difficult for pawnshops to serve as outlets for stolen merchandise.  (This was still a
concern in 1974, as indeed it had been throughout the history of
Chinese pawnbroking.)

It is difficult to determine how far this municipal intervention
was responsible for the drop in the interest rates in private pawnshops during the 1960s and early 1970s, and to what extent general
prosperity was the cause.  But the fact is that by 1965 the average
monthly rate was down to 4 percent, and by 1974 it was a mere 1.5
percent.  Private pawnbrokers' profits declined accordingly.

By all accounts, Taiwan pawnshops are readily identifiable
from the outside and at a distance,[84] as were mainland shops prior
to 1949.[85]  A cloth suspended over the main entrance bears a large
*tang* character and also expressions such as "Fair Appraisals"
(*ku-chia kung-cheng*) and "Valuables Stored in Safety" (*pao-kuan
an-ch'üan*).  Inside, the shops have counters of moderate height
with iron bars extending from countertop to ceiling, whereas
China's old pawnshops were noted for very high, but otherwise un-
protected, counters.  Personnel is scant, two or three men at most,
whereas the old shops had very large staffs.  Typical items in
pledge are television sets and motorcycles, rather than clothing,
utensils, and farming implements.

The custom of bargaining over the amount of a loan is much
as before, as is the practice of deducting the first month's interest
in advance.  The pledge period is usually set at three months,
whereas formerly it was anything from a few days to three years as
conditions varied, and could sometimes be extended--regardless of
its initial length--by renegotiation.

Lastly, it should be noted that there is an association of
pawnshops on Taiwan just as some of China's urban *tien* and *tang*
shops belonged to guilds.  In Taipei, for example, the Taipei
Pawnshop Association was formed in 1947, two years before the
Kuomintang retreat from the mainland, and consisted of a dozen
shops.  The number of members grew to 27 in 1951, 71 in 1953,
146 in 1959, and 174 in 1974.

*PART TWO*


*THE PAWNSHOP IN LATE IMPERIAL
AND REPUBLICAN TIMES*

For vivid descriptions of China during late imperial and republican times, one can do worse than to consult the journals of
little-known British travelers. In 1879, a Mrs. C. F. Gordon Cumming
was steaming upriver from the Pearl Estuary, bound for Canton,
when she wrote in her diary:

> The shores are dotted with villages, in each of
> which stands one conspicuous great solid square
> structure of granite, lined with brick, about four
> stories high. It looks like an old Border keep,
> but it really is the village pawnshop, which acts
> as the safe store-house for everybody's property.
> Here in winter are deposited all summer garments,
> and when spring returns they are reclaimed; and
> as the winter garments which are then left in pawn
> are more valuable, the owner sometimes receives
> an advance of seed for sowing his crops. Here
> there is no prejudice against the pawning of goods.
> It is a regular institution of the country, and even
> wealthy people send their goods here for safe
> keeping. Some foreigners thus dispose of their
> furs in the winter season. All goods are neatly
> packed and ticketed, and stored in pigeon-hole
> compartments of innumerable shelves, ranged tier
> above tier, to the very summit of the tall building,
> which is strongly protected both against fire and
> thieves; in fact, the latter must be mad indeed to
> face the danger of attacking a pawn-tower, on
> whose flat roof are stored not only large stones
> ready to be dropped on their devoted heads, but
> also earthenware jars full of vitriol, and syringes
> wherewith to squirt this terrible liquid fire! As
> we approached nearer and nearer to the city, the
> number of these great towers multiplied, and I am
> told that there are in Canton upwards of a hun-
> dred first class pawn-towers, besides a multitude
> of the second and third class, sufficiently proving
> how good must be their business; and it seems
> that notwithstanding the very high rate of interest
> on money lent, ranging from 20 to 36 per cent, the
> people prefer borrowing money from these brokers
> to applying to the banks. [1]

What follows in the present work, then, is a thorough discussion of what Mrs. Cumming referred to as a "first-class pawntower"; that is to say, a large *tien* or *tang* shop.[2] Since there is no study of the Chinese pawnshop in English,[3] it is to be hoped that extensive and detailed information on the subject may be found useful to students of Chinese economic and social history.

## THE LARGE CHINESE PAWNSHOP, 1875 to 1928

### Exteriors, Interiors and Fixtures

If not always a formidable "structure of granite, lined with brick," a typical *tien* or *tang* pawnshop in the period under discussion was nevertheless of considerable size and many-storied, and in villages and market towns the most imposing building in sight. It was normally square, frequently surrounded by high walls, and had windows which were always well joined, with durable frames and sills, to guard against fire and theft.[4]

Like other Chinese shops which revealed their names and specialities by means of a sign, pawnshops announced themselves with a painted signboard affixed to the outer wall. This bore a *tang* character, or a *ya* in the case of smaller shops (regardless of their particular type). Such was the practice in Shanghai, Tientsin, and Hankow, as well as in other large cities. In Canton, however, pawnshop signs either read *hsiang-ya* or *hsiang-an*;[5] and in Peking most pawnshops hung two specially constructed, greatly oversized strings of cash on either side of the entrance while the rest used a *tang*.[6]

Since pawnbroking, by its nature, was a highly specialized business, the fixtures found in pawnshops were of necessity not those employed in the usual shop. A screen, for example, was always placed just inside the front door, large enough to afford borrowers some privacy by blocking the view of curious passersby. Keeping out the noise of the marketplace so that business could be conducted in a quiet and orderly manner was also a consideration, especially when difficult appraisals had to be made, such as those involving jewelry. But the real reason for the screen, of course, was that pawning, although extremely common, was perceived to be a demeaning experience. After all, to be a customer was to admit distress. The screen was therefore primarily a face-saving fixture.[7]

Figure 1 is a schematic plan of the ground-floor interior of a large Peking pawnshop:[8]

Fig. 1. A Peking Pawnshop

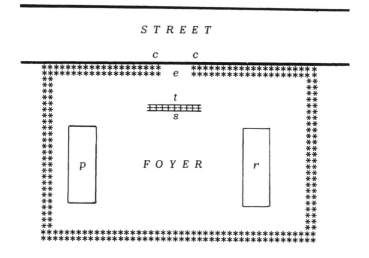

KEY:

c    large imitation string of cash
(or "*tang*" character)

e    entrance

t    "*tang*" character on screen
(used occasionally)

s    screen

p    counter for pawning

r    counter for redeeming

In pawnshops of this size, it was common for the foyer, or customer area, to be well patrolled. However, in all pawnshops, irrespective of size, counters were always high--usually six or seven feet at countertop--as a security precaution.[9] Their shape seems to have varied, some being straight and others L-shaped. This difference would hardly seem worth mentioning but for the fact that in the heyday of government financing, publicly funded *tien* shops always had straight counters while the *tang* (and smaller) shops usually had L-shaped counters, although straight ones were not unknown in them.[10] Only after public finance ceased to be a factor in pawnbroking, and *tien* and *tang* shops became difficult to distinguish, were counters of both shapes used interchangeably, the considerations then being merely those of interior design and floor space.

Storage was a problem facing all pawnshops, since various kinds of articles had to be put away not only in safety but also sometimes over long periods. In a large shop, after an item had been pledged, it was either shelved upstairs or, in the case of jewelry, placed in special container cabinets that were kept in the room of the "safekeeper of valuables."[11]

Shelves made from wood, preferably pine for durability, and generally installed in the floors immediately above the shop, were used for most belongings left in pawn.[12] Standing in rows far enough apart to afford easy access to pawnshop personnel, such shelves were divided into pigeon-holes (that were normally about two feet high, three feet wide and seventeen inches deep) and were supported at fixed intervals by posts to which bamboo strips were attached. These strips bore code numbers that matched those entered in a series of ledgers.

The container cabinets were likewise made of wood. Although their size was not uniform, they all had built-in drawers to keep jewelry in relative safety. These drawers were coded in a manner identical to that used in marking the sections of the shelf.

Two requirements for the interiors of large pawnshops were sufficient circulation of fresh air and proper lighting. Since Chinese pawnshops traditionally functioned not only as places of pawning but also as places of storage, pawnbrokers were concerned to preserve in good condition all items deposited in trust. The circulation of fresh air was vital to prevent damage from damp, mildew, and insects to articles such as silk clothing and good quality furs. Neglect in this area could cause a pawnbroker severe loss.

Inadequate lighting could also cause losses. This was especially true in the large urban pawnshops, where a higher percentage of goods received had substantial value. If, as a result of insufficient lighting, a faulty appraisal was made and pearls or

precious stones were overvalued, or fake jewelry passed off as
genuine, a pawnbroker's loss could be heavy, since under such
circumstances the borrower was certain not to return to redeem his
goods, but merely to pocket the money loaned.[13]

Additional comments on<br>
Tien, Tang, Ya and Tai-tang

As already mentioned, the distinction between various types
of pawnshops was often blurred. There were, however, some clear-
cut differences. One of them was that a *tien* shop's resources were
usually great enough to allow it to enter into very large pawning
transactions, virtually without an upper limit (such as in the case
of very rare stones), while the other shops did set ceilings on the
size of the pledge and the amount of money they would lend on it at
interest. Thus, the latter on occasion found themselves in the position of having to refuse a transaction.

There was a difference, too, in the amount of the license fee.
In Kiangsu province during the period under discussion, for example, a *ya*-type pawnshop paid only 100 *yüan* per annum and a *chih*
shop 300 *yüan*, while a *tang* shop paid 500 *yüan*. A similar scale
was established for contributions to the public welfare, charities,
and so on (although such contributions appear not to have been
mandatory). It was often difficult, however, to assess a pawnshop
fairly and thus require of it the appropriate license fee, because
*tien* and *tang* shops sometimes masqueraded as *ya* shops.[14]
Besides the obvious advantages of paying less tax, a lower license
fee and a smaller amount in contributions, the main reason for such
a strategem seems to have been a regulation made by the industry
itself, sometimes promulgated through the pawnshop trade associations, that a *tien* or *tang* proprietor would not establish his shop
within a radius of one hundred households from another.[15] Since
no such restriction pertained to *ya* (or *chih*) shops, a proprietor
wishing to encroach on another pawnbroker's territory simply
called this new shop a *ya*. Once again, what should have been a
clear-cut distinction proved difficult to draw.

An additional comment relating to the *tai-tang* should be made.
Under Kuomintang rule, when there was a movement of *tien* and
*tang* shops back to rural areas, often in the guise of *tai-tang* to
evade taxation, there was at the same time a legitimate use of surplus *tien* and *tang* capital generated in urban areas. A shop, in a
favorable financial position yet unable to expand its business premises or unwilling to flaunt trade regulations, channeled its excess
funds into *tai-tang*, setting up in effect branch locations.

*Tien* and *Tang* Pawnshop Organization

Capital Organization

In the period under review, *tien* and *tang* ownership usually took the form of a limited partnership, although many *tien* and *tang* shops financed by a single person or family survived from earlier times. When the assets of a given shop only ranged from several ten thousand *yüan* up to several hundred thousand *yüan*, group ownership was the exception. The problem with single ownership was of course the unlimited liability that went with it in cases of damage or destruction of pledged articles by fire or other means. In a partnership, each partner's liability was limited to his share of of the business.[16] It was for the reason of extra protection, then, that most of the large and more recently established *tien* and *tang* pawnshops were limited partnerships.

Following modern business practice, shares in shops were acknowledged in a contract, a copy of which was retained by each party after its execution as a proof of the ownership of said shares.[17] The contract also stipulated how profits and losses were to be dealt with and laid down procedures governing the withdrawal of shares and addition of capital, the times of shareholders' meetings, and other business matters.[18] Capital in limited partnership pawnshops was usually organized in blocks of several ten thousand *yüan*, the basic unit being ten thousand *yüan*. Total capital depended on the size and scale of a particular shop and reflected the level of population and commerce in its location. If it were not sufficiently large and could not meet the needs of the community, a pawnshop ran the risk of having to stop business.[19]

Internal Organization

Once the capital for a limited partnership pawnshop had been accumulated, the owners of a new *tien* or *tang* shop were faced with the task of setting up its internal organization, which was a rather complicated procedure. This organizational structure had to be reported to the local authorities in a document called a "tien certificate" (*tien-t'ieh*), which also had to list all the contracted conditions of the partnership as well as information relating to the petitioning of the appropriate government office for registration and the application for a business license. Having completed the above and opened the pawnshop for business, there was, finally, the responsibility of paying tax in monthly installments.[20]

What was the internal organization of a typical *tien* or *tang* shop? In general, it was divided into four sections under a manager (*ching-li* or *kuan-shih*), who was of course answerable to the shareholders (*ku-tung*). The sections were: "business" (*ying-yeh*), "safekeeping of valuables" (*pao-kuan*), "receipts and expenditures" (*ch'u-na*), and "accounting" (*k'uai-chi*). In the pawnbroking trade, however, they were not referred to under these names. The business section was called "outer posts" (*wai-ch'üeh*) and the three remaining sections collectively "inner posts" (*nei-ch'üeh*). There were also the so-called "middle posts" (*chung-ch'üeh*) and the "student-apprentices" (*hsüeh-sheng*). As the personnel organizational chart on page 27 indicates, the structure was very complicated.21

*The Manager.* A *tien* or *tang* pawnshop manager was normally selected by the shareholders and entrusted with running the shop, including its financial management and intra-industry affairs. Thus, a manager was usually a capable man who had devoted his entire working life to pawnbroking and enjoyed a good business reputation.

*The Public Relations Officer (wai-hsi).* This was a special position in that although its occupant was beneath the manager in rank, he was not under the manager's control. The public relations officer was selected by shareholders and was responsible for all external affairs other than business matters, such as dealings with government officers, guilds, unions and associations. It was he who entertained when necessary on behalf of the pawnshop and solved community relations problems.22 There were cases--in the smaller-scale *tien* and *tang* shops--where the manager himself assumed the role of public relations officer.

*Business Personnel (ying-yeh yüan) (Outer Posts).* It appears that traditionally pawnshops had one counter opposite the main entrance (unlike the Peking pawnshop, illustrated on page 22 above, in which there were two counters, one for pawning and one for redeeming). Behind it stood the head counterman (*shou-kuei*) to the far right, with the second, third and fourth countermen (*erh-kuei, san-kuei* and *szu-kuei*) to his left, as shown in Figure 2. The head counterman was directly opposite the door and was therefore in the most prominent position.23

Three points should be made regarding pawnshop countermen. The first two deal with their responsibilities for the receipt of pawned items and issuing funds at interest and for the collection of interest payments. Countermen were worth nothing unless they could: (1) give proper appraisals, that is, determine the authenticity and probable resale price of valuable objects;24 and (2) calculate interest correctly, since in the case of error in favor of the borrower, there was of course no way to recoup the loss.

Chart 1. Internal Organization of a *Tien* or *Tang* Pawnshop

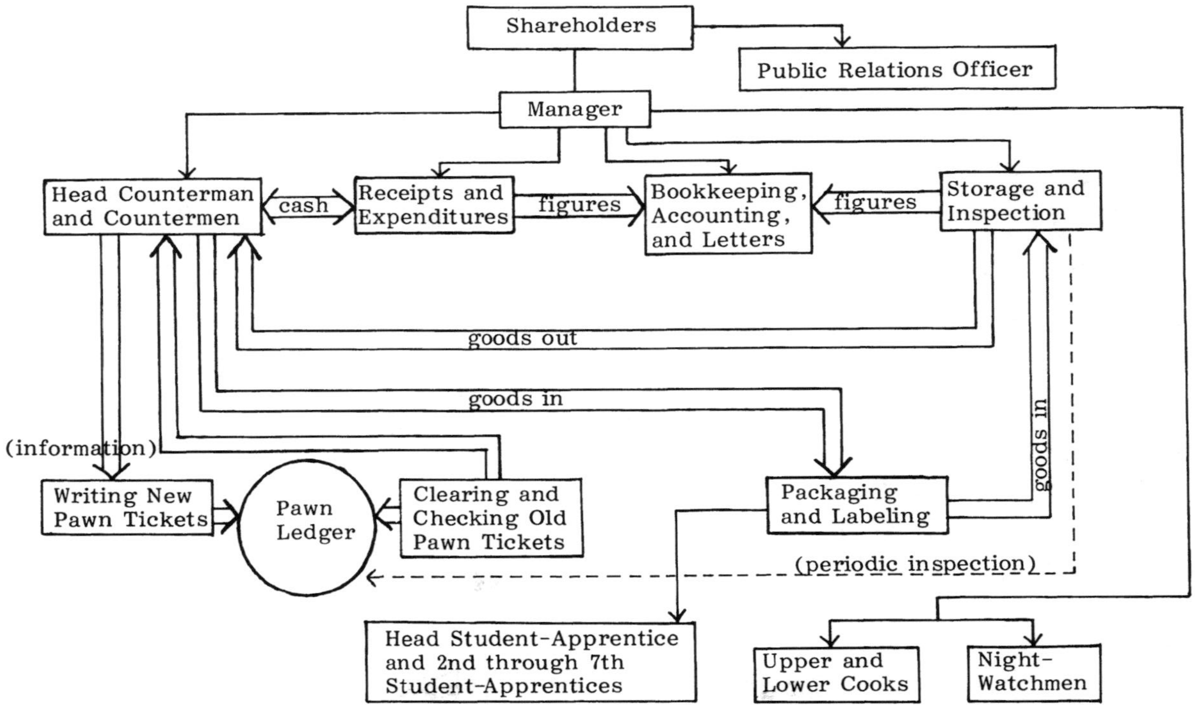

Fig. 2. A Traditional Pawnshop

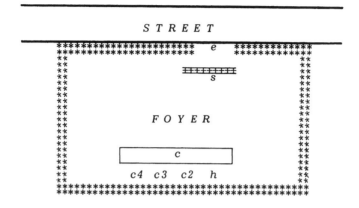

KEY:

e   entrance

s   screen

c   counter

h   head counterman

c2,c3,c4   countermen

The third point concerns the attitude of countermen in dealing with customers. In the pawnbroking trade, it was considered good business practice for countermen always to be friendly and courteous. Periods of severe competition were not infrequent, and any discourtesy shown during a pawning transaction might drive a customer to another shop in the future.[25]

Finally, it should be noted that each counterman, regardless of rank, worked on his own, completing all tasks by himself; a single transaction was never divided among two or more countermen. During slack periods, a particular borrower might well do business with the head counterman, if he were not occupied, merely because of his prominent position opposite the entrance. But pawnshops were often scenes of chaos, their foyers crammed with customers, especially at the end of the year. During periods of crisis, too, there were frequent runs on pawnshops as there were on banks. At these times, all countermen were equally busy and, by necessity, functioned autonomously.

*Managerial Personnel (kuan-li yüan) (Inner Posts).* Little need be said about the person in charge of wrapping (*kuan-pao*) and the person in charge of valuables (*kuan-shih*). Although the former did not do the actual packaging himself, he had to be able to supervise the wrapping of a sometimes bewildering array of items--clothing, bronzeware, copperware, tinware, and the like. Since he was responsible for the safekeeping of these items, and they were always stored upstairs, he was sometimes known as the "upstairs manager"(*kuan-lou*).[26]

The duties of the person in charge of funds (*kuan-ch'ien*) were many and various. Every morning he handed a sufficient amount of money to the countermen for use in loaning throughout the business day. In the evening, at closing time, he took back what they had received in principal and interest payments from borrowers redeeming items. He was also responsible for money paid out and taken in by each section of the pawnshop and for doing its banking. Finally, he kept a daily record of cash flow.

The accountant (*kuan-chang*) had to transfer to the general ledger all the transactions recorded by the person in charge of funds and to compile monthly business reports based on them. He also handled all business dealings with banks and money shops and thus settled outside accounts. Furthermore, he took care of the pawnshop's correspondence.[27]

*Middle Posts.* Middle posts took their name from their place in the organizational scheme beneath the outer and inner posts but above the lowly student-apprentices. There were four such posts: ticket-writer, ticket-checker, the wrapper, and the person in charge of labeling and storage.

The writing of pawn tickets was a specialty. When a counterman completed a transaction, he literally sang out a description of
the item or items pawned and the amount of money advanced on
pledge.[28] Listening carefully in the rear of the shop, the ticket-
writer entered this information in a pawn ledger and on the pawn
ticket itself. He then placed the ticket next to the ledger entry and
affixed a "ch'i-feng" seal.[29,30] This having been done, the ticket
was handed to the borrower who was required to present it when he
redeemed his pledge. The next chore of the writer was to assign a
code number to each item and note the date of receipt. Needless to
say, he not only had to have a keen ear for this job but an extremely
rapid writing brush as well.

The clearing and checking of pawn tickets occurred when a
borrower returned to redeem his pledge. The person in the pawnshop responsible for this task took the ticket and matched it by code
number against the appropriate entry in the pawn ledger for purposes of verification. Every ten days the person in charge of
wrapping examined this ledger, thereby determining the accuracy
of the person doing the abovementioned matching, and affixed a
seal opposite each transaction completed during the period. If the
pawn period on an item had expired and there was no seal to show
that it had been redeemed, then it was set aside to be auctioned off
by the pawnshop. Matching and arranging of returned tickets in
sequence and by code number was therefore of prime importance.

Storage by correct code number was equally important. Otherwise, locating an item on the shelves or in the jewelry container
cabinets would have been impossible. Proper packaging was also
an aid to reliable and orderly storage. There were two men responsible for this area of operation.[31] One man was a packager, whose
aims were neatness and compactness--the first to avoid damage, the
second to economize on shelf space. Clothing, silks, and cotton
cloth were folded, wrapped, and tied in a prescribed manner, the
end result being the trimmest possible bundle. The other man, in
charge of labeling and storage, wrote the code number, a description of the contents, the number of items, and the money advanced
on pledge, as clearly as possible on a strip of bamboo or wood
usually two feet long by one inch wide and attached it to the top of
the packager's bundle.[32]

*Student-Apprentices.* At the foot of the organizational ladder, the student-apprentices normally underwent a very long and
sometimes exacting service, during which time they were supposed
in theory to study all aspects of pawnbroking, but in fact merely
fetched and carried for senior personnel. Ranking was in accordance with date of entry into the pawnshop, and promotion was always step-by-step.

*Cooks (shang-tsao, hsia-tsao) and Night Watchmen (keng-fu).*
While cooks and night watchmen were not considered part of a
pawnshop's organization, they were nevertheless under the direct
supervision of the manager. There were two grades of cooks: the
"upper cooks" (*shang-tsao*), who prepared food for the manager and
top business and managerial personnel, and the "lower cooks" (*hsia-
tsao*), who cooked for the middle posts and student-apprentices.

## Business

### Trade Regulations (*yeh-kuei*)

The "New Pawnshop Industry Regulations," issued by the
Kiangsu Province Department of Finance in 1927, give valuable guid-
ance as to the rights and privileges pawnbroking enjoyed and the
degree of government control under which it had to operate. The
history of these regulations is also of some interest. Evidently
stemming from customary and unwritten pawnbroking business practices prevalent in the Ch'ing dynasty, a set of so-called *Mu-pang
kuei-t'iao* (literally "Regulations Posted on Wooden Signboards") was
promulgated in Kiangsu in late imperial times. It was superseded in
the early years of the Republic (1913) by another set of regulations,
the "Revised Pawnshop *Mu-pang kuei-t'iao.*" This set was submit-
ted in a petition to the provincial department of finance, which
transmitted it to the provincial governor for registration, who in
turn issued an order to all pawnshops to abide by it. The "New
Pawnshop Industry Regulations" of 1927 were drafted and put into
law in an effort to root out inequities to both pawnbroker and
borrower contained in the 1913 set. The protests raised against
the new regulations in the following year by the Kiangsu pawnbrokers when they met in Nanking, and their request to retain the
regulations of 1913, suggest that they considered the borrower's
position to have become too advantageous. To some extent, therefore, the 1927 regulations may not give a wholly accurate picture of
earlier practices. An abridged version of these regulations follows.

### New Pawnshop Industry Regulations
(winter, 1927)

1. Merchants with joint or individual capital who . . . wish to open
   a pawnshop may do so upon verification of capital assets by the
   government and upon issuance of a certificate.

2. The monetary standard for the exchange of pawned items shall
   be the silver dollar. Copper coins must be valued at the day's

market rate, which must be clearly displayed in front of the counter. Pawnbrokers are forbidden to impose charges other than regular interest. Depositors shall be free to choose whether or not their pledges are boxed for storage.[33]

3.  The valuation of a pledge shall be fair. To transact business by coercion or on the pawner's word alone (regarding the value of the item) is forbidden.

4.  Goods that can be proved to be government property, or that are so rare and unusual that they cannot be valued, should be refused as pledges.

5.  A pawnbroker whose fully subscribed original capital is insufficient may be permitted on verification by the authorities to suspend business temporarily and resume it after raising further capital.

6.  The interest charged by a pawnbroker may not exceed two percent per month.

7.  Because eighteen months constitute the full pledge period, items in pawn which have not been redeemed at the end of that time may be sold off.

8.  Pawnshops are permitted to charge interest by the month. Should the first month pass and an item be redeemed within the first five days of the next month, no interest may be charged for this second month. . . . During October and November, cotton clothing and blankets can be used instead of cash for interest payments; during February and March, farm implements can be used to pay interest.[34]

9.  A borrower may not redeem a portion of items originally pledged as a "lot," but must redeem the entire "lot" at one time, or not at all.[35]

10. A borrower who does not wish to pawn an item for the full pledge period may pay interest on a month-to-month basis, depending on how long the item is kept.

11. In the case of war, theft, vandalism, flood, fire or *"force majeure,"* there is no need whatever for a pawnbroker to indemnify. After verification of a particular disaster by local government agencies or community organizations, however, undamaged items with recognizable markings, or with attached pawn code numbers, may be redeemed as usual. Items which are damaged or bear no identifiable marks . . . are to be sold, half of the amount of sale to accrue to the pawnbroker and half to be

divided among the borrowers proportionately to the value of their tickets.

12. If an item is lost because of theft or carelessness on the part of pawnshop personnel, a local government arbitrator will be called in to investigate. He will calculate the average value of all items sold at auction within the previous two years by the pawnshop in question and decide on a figure for the purpose of indemnification. The money already advanced by the pawnshop on the missing item as well as interest charges will be deducted from this figure. . . .

    1) If loss is due to theft, the amount of compensation shall be equal to the full acknowledged price of the item on the pawn ticket.

    2) If loss is due to carelessness, then the amount of compensation shall be equal to half of the acknowledged price shown on the pawn ticket.

13. If a thief pawns stolen items, and their rightful owner files a complaint with the officials, who in turn, upon suitable proof, issue him a document of ownership, he can redeem the said items . . . but he does not need to pay the interest charges. When the thief is caught, the officials can recover the amount of pledge and return it to the owner. . . .

14. If a borrower loses his pawn ticket, he must report its loss to the pawnshop, together with its description, date of issue, and the amount of money advanced on the item itself. The borrower must also find a reputable shop in the area [that is, a *regular* shop, not a pawnshop] to act as his guarantor, and at the same time he must file a "lost pawn ticket" report with the local headman. If the pawnshop's own investigation confirms this report, the pawnbroker may issue a new ticket to the borrower, who must first pay the interest in full. If the case is not entirely clear, or if there is no surety, the pawnbroker does not have to replace the lost pawn ticket.

15. When matching a pawn ticket against its corresponding entry in the pawn ledger by means of the *"ch'i-feng"* seal, if a forgery is detected or there has been an attempt at defacing or alteration, then the ticket is to be considered null and void, and a case will be brought and prosecuted according to law.

Regional and Seasonal Variations

    *Items Pawned.* Pawnshops received many types of articles in pledge. The key to the frequency with which a particular article was used as collateral for a loan was pawnshop location. In more prosperous urban areas where the large *tien* and *tang* shops were found, gold and silver, pearls and precious stones were the most common items pawned, and furs and pelts only slightly less so. Cloth garments were more rare, and wooden utensils, copperware and tinware rarer still.

Rural areas presented the picture practically in reverse. The most frequently pledged articles were ironware, that is, ploughs and hoes, and also anchors in the vicinity of inland waterways. Garments, copperware and tinware were less often seen, and jewelry of any description was almost never pawned.

*Pawning Patterns.* The pawnshop in the period under review was a major factor in the circulation of money. It tended to pump money into the economy during periods of cash scarcity and siphon it off when there was a surplus. Since farmers planted in the spring and harvested in the fall, pawnbrokers, broadly speaking, pawned in the spring, when farmers were short of funds, and redeemed in the fall, when farmers had a cash surplus.

Pawnbrokers also pawned rather than redeemed prior to the New Year, and in fact, reached their greatest volume of pawning at that time, because Chinese custom had long decreed that all outstanding debts be settled by the end of the year. [36]

Pawnbrokers also responded to other fluctuations. February and March witnessed the beginning of the tea market, for example, and there was a corresponding demand for cash. Similarly, the silk market started in April and May, with the same result. Consequently, pawnbroking did well during these months. June, on the other hand, was a hot month and a sluggish time for business (*ch'ing-shui liu-yüeh*, "the unmuddied waters of the sixth moon," was a common phrase for this period), and pawnbroking suffered accordingly. This slack season continued throughout the summer as the crops ripened. Following the autumn rush to redeem, there was a second leveling off in the volume of pawnshop business during October and November. [37]

December and January, as mentioned above, marked the pawnbroking industry's busiest time, when pawnshops were said to "swarm like the marketplace." [38] "So many customers squeezed their way through the doors that employees behind the counters had difficulty in handling the volume of business, while beyond the counters people milled around in confusion like tangled strands of silk. From sunrise to sunset, there was no respite. During the days remaining until the end of the year, the pace became even more frantic, as people flocked to the pawnshops in ever increasing numbers. On New Year's Eve itself, neither urban nor rural pawnbroker shut his door. There was confusion everywhere, and clerks remained on duty all night to serve customers, who only began to dwindle away at the dawn of the New Year."[39]

*Interest Rates and Pledge Periods.* Mention has already been made in Part One of the trend to increasingly lower rates of interest per pledge period over the fifteen hundred years that pawnbroking was known to China. The trend was also towards shorter pledge periods, so that the true annual rate fell much less sharply.[40] For the period 1875 to 1928, there were wide variations both in interest levels and pledge period lengths. There were also seasonal fluctuations in interest rates as well as different rates for different items pawned.

In late imperial times, interest rates in southern Kiangsu fell steadily from 30 to 20 percent due to recovery from the Taiping Rebellion,[41] while the pledge period remained fixed at eighteen months. Subsequently, interest rates in the Shanghai area fell to 16 percent, but the prevailing rates in Wusih, Ch'ang-chou, Chenchiang, Yang-chou and Nan-t'ung stayed at 20 percent. In areas north of the Yangtze and Huai rivers, and in counties along the Huai itself, interest rates held at about 25 percent. At the same time, 20 to 30 percent interest was common for a two-year pledge period in the Peking-Tientsin area, while Hupeh pawnshops exacted 30 to 50 percent for only a sixteen-month pledge period. When Chang Chih-tung was appointed governor-general of Hu-kuang (i.e., Hunan and Hupeh) in 1889, however, he ordered all Hupeh pawnbrokers to lower interest rates to 20 percent and increase the pledge period to a uniform twenty months.

There was an effort under the Republic to reduce interest rates throughout China, but this did not always achieve the desired result. Pawnbrokers often cut the pledge period in direct proportion to the amount of reduction in the interest. There were even pawnbrokers who had pledged at 25 percent for sixteen months in 1917 and 1918, but who pledged at the same rate in 1921 for a mere twelve months.

Pawnbrokers sometimes lowered lending rates during slack business times, such as the winters in northern China, for example, and the summer doldrums mentioned earlier. All of them lowered rates at the end of the year "out of kindness to the poor."[42] On the sixteenth of November, full pledge period interest rates of 30 percent were reduced to 20, and those of 20 to 15 percent. On the second of January of the New Year, however, these rates were brought back to their former levels.

Some pawnshops charged interest on a sliding scale, depending on the size and value of an item. If a certain article required a great deal of shelf space, interest on it might be higher than on another article of equal value but more compact and easily wrapped. As a rule, the lower the value of a pledge, the higher the interest on it. The most unfavorable interest rates were those given to pledges that were both of little value and bulky, such as farm implements.

### Hours of Pawnshop Operation

Pawnbroking hours differed from province to province. Most pawnshops opened for business at seven or eight o'clock in the morning and closed at six or seven in the evening. In the treaty ports, some pawnshops did not shut their doors until nine o'clock at night. As a rule, all pawnshops opened for only half a day on national holidays and festivals, but on New Year's Eve, of course, they never closed. [43]

### Turnover of Capital

Since the pawnbroking industry's income was almost totally derived from interest, it might seem that the higher the interest, for given operating costs, the greater the profit. Such, however, was not the case. The key prerequisite for large profits was the rapid turnover of capital, or, in other words, fast redemptions. Pawnbrokers who had to "wait out" full pledge periods, or who were forced to sell unredeemed items after the expiration of the pledge term in order to recoup a percentage of their cash outlay, were in trouble because the true annual return on the capital involved was thereby reduced. The fewer items left for the full pledge period, the better it was for the pawnbroker. [44]

### Sale of Full-Term Items

During the period under discussion, and in fact much earlier, pawnshops conducted regular spring and autumn sales of unre- deemed articles (called *hsia-chia* and *ta-tang*). Jewelers, silver- smiths and goldsmiths would undertake to buy *objets précieux*, and wholesalers and clothing stores would arrange to purchase goods. Pawnshops sold such goods in lots (*tzu-hao*). Although each lot was bound to contain items of varying degrees of quality, every article in it was considered to have the same value, which was equal to the average amount advanced on pledge (an amount far below the average real value). Thus, a price per unit multiplied by the number of units would give the base--or "break even"-- price of a lot (not unlike the reserve sale price at an auction). Traditionally, pawnshops did not let the lots go at this figure but marked it up 10 percent (*kua-i*) or 20 percent (*kua-erh*) when offering them for sale. In the 1920s, however, when the clothing industry fell on hard times, goods lots, far from being marked up, had to be discounted 10 or 20 percent if pawnshops were to dispose of them. There were even instances when averaging the value of all items in lots was no longer acceptable to wholesalers and clothing stores, and some articles had to be sold at below the amount advanced on pledge (this "markdown" was termed *k'uei-hao*, literally, "a loss 'lot'").

Unfavorable as these conditions were, the pawnshop was in a better position than some other financial institutions, which loaned money entirely on credit; at least it had collateral in the form of mortgaged items. Even if it did not recoup its full cash outlay and interest foregone, it could get rid of the items at biannual sales and so recover the greater part of its investment.

Troublesome Areas

Rapid changes in clothing styles, which caused garments to lose most of their value during the term of their pledge, have already been discussed.

Another area of difficulty for the pawnbroker was the appraisal of jewelry and gold (quite apart from the problem of erroneously accepting "fakes" or imitation jewelry as genuine). In the case of jewelry, it was a question of "striking a balance" with a customer. If the pawnbroker's appraisal was too low, the customer would take his business elsewhere; if it was too high, the pawnbroker ran a great risk, because, in the event of resale at the expiration of the pledge period, he could suffer an enormous loss. The risks with gold were even greater, since its value was tied to the world market price, over which the Chinese pawnbroker exerted no control whatsoever. During the First World War, for example, gold prices fell sharply, and no gold in pawn was redeemed.

Tight money markets were another concern. In such markets, interest rates soared while pawnshop rates were fixed by regulation. Although they could be--and were--lowered periodically as an incentive to borrowers during certain seasons, they could not be raised above the statutory level.

Currency devaluation could also spell disaster for a pawnshop. In 1927, for instance, devaluation in Wuhan was so rapid that in a matter of months the city was flooded with paper money. During August and September, borrowers rushed the pawnshops and redeemed every item on their shelves for a fraction of their

real value. Unlike regular shops faced with similar conditions,
pawnshops could not resort to the retail markup.

Finally, rises in the cost of living in the form of higher wages
affected pawnshops more than regular shops because of the comparatively large sizes of their staffs.[45]

## Management

### Management of Personnel

Regulations concerning pawnshop personnel were normally
posted on a sign which was displayed in the main working area for
all to see. Some of the more important provisions were as follows.

*Firing of Employees.* As a rule, pawnshops fired personnel
only on the fifth or seventh of January. A discharged employee
had to be off the premises by the evenings of those days. Under
no circumstances could he stay the night.

*Movement of Employees.* Unless their family lived locally, all
personnel had to sleep on the premises. If they left during the
day, they had to return by midnight. If they carried a wrapped
parcel out of the pawnshop, its contents had to be inspected by
more than one person--a provision that was doubtless designed not
only to avoid theft but also collusion. Lastly, student-apprentices
were forbidden to leave the pawnshop except on those festival days
when it kept short business hours. The only exception to this rule
occurred when a student-apprentice had a letter from a parent or
relative (presumably bringing news of illness, injury, or death in
the family).

*Employee Compensation to the Pawnshop for the Acceptance of
Counterfeit Items.* According to Yang Chao-yü, "Whenever an
employee receives an item in pawn and inspection proves it to be
counterfeit, he must pay the pawnshop for the loss himself. . . ."
This provision is difficult to justify. The tenor of Yang's previous
remarks on counterfeit items seems to suggest that countermen
(the only personnel who would receive such items) were not indivi-
dually responsible for an error in judgment and that resulting
losses would be absorbed by the pawnshop. There is the point too
that a transaction involving a counterfeit would no doubt mean an
advance of a substantial amount of money, and that conceivably a
counterman might have to give up years of his salary in making
good the loss.[46]

*Overdrawing.* An employee was neither allowed to borrow money from a pawnshop nor to receive his wages in advance.

*Conduct.* There was a prohibition against unseemly behavior; and gambling, smoking opium, and the like were expressly forbidden.

Naturally, the pawnshop manager shouldered complete responsibility for management. Personnel could also supervise all persons beneath them on the organizational chart, so that the student-apprentices were "used" by everybody, though by pawnshop custom they were under the control of the person in charge of wrapping.

Pawnshop employees had a statutory holiday of two months a year.[47] If in a given year an employee did not request a vacation, he was often able to accumulate the time and apply it to the following year. By regulation, however, all employees had to return to the pawnshop at the end of the year, unless there were extenuating circumstances. (It will be recalled that the end of the year marked the peak business period, and all hands were needed.) For their first three years as trainees, student-apprentices could not stipulate the time of their holidays (which could be one or two months in length) but took them whenever it suited management.

Daily and Periodic Routines

Pawnshops opened their doors at seven or eight o'clock in the morning, at which time the person in charge of funds distributed money to the countermen for use during the day.

Each counterman in a *tien* or *tang* shop kept his own ledger (*ts'ao-pu*) and entered the amounts of money disbursed in loans and taken in for redemptions. Thus, when an item was pawned, he recorded the amount of the pledge; and when an article was redeemed, he noted the principal and interest paid in. At closing time in the evening, he totaled the day's accounts and then took all the cash to the person in charge of funds, who made the appropriate entry in the journal (*liu-shui pu*) and checked the counterman's ledger for error. If there was a shortage, the counterman was automatically responsible for making good the deficit.

Also at the end of the day, the persons in charge of wrapping and valuables compared the descriptions attached to items taken in that day with the corresponding entries in the pawn ledger (*tang-pu*) to make sure they matched. It was the function of the student-apprentices to read aloud the package tags and ledger entries to these managerial personnel. Once it had been established that there were no mistakes, the student-apprentices stamped the ledger entries with the seals "Put Upstairs" (*ju-lou*) or "Put in Jewelry Box" (*ju-shih*), as required. They then took the packages upstairs for storage on the code-numbered shelves. But it was the person in charge of valuables himself who placed the wrapped jewelry in the container cabinets.

The accountant meanwhile totaled the amount of money advanced on pledge during the day to see whether it corresponded with the various totals in the countermen's individual ledgers.

When an item was redeemed, a counterman received a pawn ticket (*tang-p'iao*) from the borrower who had returned to redeem his pledge. He then calculated interest charges and noted them on the ticket, so that in the evening the person in charge of wrapping could reexamine it for error and make a correction if necessary. Next he entered the transaction in his own ledger and gave the ticket to a student-apprentice, who entered its code number and the amount of pledge money in a "registration ledger" (*kua-hao pu*). Then, with ticket in hand, the student-apprentice rushed upstairs to search for the appropriate item according to its code number. While he was thus occupied, the counterman downstairs took in the principal and interest due from the borrower.

When the student-apprentice returned with the packaged article, it was unwrapped and inspected by the counterman; and if there was no mistake, it was returned to the borrower. The pawn ticket was transferred to the person in charge of clearing and checking pawn tickets (*ch'ing-p'iao che*), a "middle post" whose task it was to enter the code number and the amount of the pledge in a "cancellation ledger" (*ts'ao-hsiao pu*), so that his entry could be compared against that of the counterman and thus eliminate errors.

At closing time, it was the duty of the person in charge of wrapping to check the registration ledger against the cancellation ledger and affix a seal bearing the characters *tui-t'ung* ("matched and agreed to") on top of the correct entries.

The abovementioned cross-checks in the pawning and redeeming procedures, occurring as they did at virtually every step, made the commission of mistakes, and indeed fraud, extremely difficult.

Every ten days, it was the responsibility of the person in charge of clearing and checking to arrange by code number the pawn tickets received during that period and to make a fair copy of his findings. Then the person in charge of wrapping had to match the tickets against the pawn ledger, certifying entries with a *ch'ü-yin* seal (signifying redemption).[48]

A pawnshop took a thorough inventory every year. All items in the pawn ledger not stamped with the *ch'ü-yin* seal were tallied against every item entered in a so-called "shelf ledger."[49] It appears that this inventory was very painstaking, and no discrepancies were permitted. Normally carried out at the beginning of winter, it had the twin virtues of getting the pawnshop in order prior to the year-end rush and of preparing in part for the year-end business reckoning.

Pawnshop staff packaged garments in certain prescribed ways. Cloth garments were generally rolled into bundles, whereas silks, satins and furs were usually "boxed" (*ts'un-hsiang*). This did not in fact involve placing these expensive items in boxes for storage, but rather folding them neatly and wrapping them in durable paper made from the paper-mulberry tree. Clothing with a pawn value of $5.00 or more had to be boxed. If the value was less than $5.00, the borrower could have it boxed if he wished, but there was a charge which amounted to 1 or 2 percent of the money advanced on pledge. When this occurred, a "boxed" seal was stamped both on the pawn ticket and in the pawn ledger.

The business of a lost pawn ticket was a complicated one, with potentially serious ramifications for the pawnshop. Since pawning was done anonymously, no personal identification was required from the borrower, and it was thus impossible to match him to the item redeemed by any means other than a pawn ticket. The fears, therefore, were two: (1) that a misplaced or stolen ticket might be brought to the pawnshop by a third person for the purpose of redeeming an article; and (2) that a third person might know of or memorize the description of a valuable item in pawn and register a false pawn ticket loss.

Such actions were not discovered until the appearance of the true borrower, usually much later on. If a stolen ticket was presented, the only remedy was the arrest of the thief. If a false claim of a lost pawn ticket was made, a guarantor, without whom no substitute ticket could be issued, and of whose trustworthiness the employee registering the lost ticket claim had to be personally satisfied, was held liable by the pawnshop.

If the pawnshop agreed to accept a borrower's registration of loss, it issued him, on special white paper, a handwritten ticket that could not be mistaken for a regular printed one in a procedure known as *pu-p'iao* ("replacing the ticket"). Its issue immediately invalidated the lost original ticket, should it be subsequently found.

Since this lost pawn ticket procedure caused the pawnshop to conduct an in-house investigation, a fee equal to 10 percent of the pledge money was charged. If the amount advanced was very large, the borrower could bargain with the pawnshop employee who was handling the matter in an effort to reduce this charge. Such a reduction was up to the employee himself, because money realized by the charge did not figure in the profits of the pawnshop but was rather considered as the direct income of the employee in question.

## The Pawnshop Accounting System

### Business Pawn Tickets and Ledgers

*Pawn Tickets.* Traditionally student-apprentices had printed pawn tickets themselves on the shop premises. But such printing was usually of poor quality, and during the period under review the job was given to professional printers subject to stringent guarantees.[50] The ticket bore the name of the pawnshop,[51] its address, the phrases "Mortgage Time Limit" and "Interest Calculation" followed by spaces, and a disclaimer of responsibility for damage caused by insects, moths, mildew or damp.[52]

At the upper right-hand corner of a pawn ticket there was a code number, which consisted of one character and a number. The character came from the *Ch'ien-tzu wen* (*The Thousand Character Classic*, in which no character is ever repeated) and served as a given month's standard code element. The next character in the *Ch'ien-tzu wen* was used the following month, and so on, month after month. The number "1" marked the first item pawned during the given month; and since pawned articles were numbered consecutively as well as recorded in numerical sequence, it was always possible to determine the number of transactions at the end of the month. Coding began anew each month with the number "1." In this manner, no two pawn tickets from the same pawnshop could bear identical code numbers unless the *Ch'ien-tzu wen* had been exhausted, which would have taken more than eighty-three years.

Beneath the code number, the right-hand column on a pawn ticket was used for listing the type of item(s) being pawned, as well as their description and number. At the top of the middle column were the characters *tang-pen*, or "money advanced on pledge." In the left-hand column, the date of the pawning transaction was recorded.

Due to limitations of space on the pawn ticket itself, it was often the practice of countermen to spread the transaction over several tickets, if many kinds of articles were pledged at one time by a single borrower. This especially applied when jewelry (kept in container cabinets in the custody of the person in charge of valuables) was pawned with goods to be shelved upstairs. Regardless of the types of items involved, this practice was also a convenience to the borrower making a large pledge. Should he wish to redeem part of it, having it spread over several pawn tickets enabled him to skirt the recent provision that individual articles could not be redeemed from "lots" (see the Kiangsu "Regulations," number nine on page 32 above).

*The Pawn Ledger* (also called *tien-chang*). The pawn ledger was the principal accounting tool of the pawnbroking industry. It was more than one foot square, and each of its double pages contained ten vertical columns. Every page was divided horizontally into four sections: the first, or top, section contained the code number; the second, the borrower's "surname," which was a fiction, for even if a counterman knew a borrower personally, a *wang* character was habitually used; the third, and by far the largest, section on the page noted the types, descriptions and number of articles pledged; and the fourth, or bottom, section was used for entering the amount of the advance. A new pawn ledger was begun each month, and at the end of the year, all twelve ledgers were bound into a single volume.

At the conclusion of a transaction, and after the pawn ticket and pawn ledger had both been filled in, the ticket's right edge was placed over the matching ledger entry and stamped with the *ch'i-feng* seal which carried the four-character phrase *chu-lien pi-ho*, literally, "matching pearls and jades," thus meaning "matching exactly" or "no breaking point."

*The Counterman's Account Book or Ledger.* This book was generally quite broad and squat, and was so arranged that totals of money advanced and money received could be separated for convenient end-of-the-day tally with the pawn ledger and the cancellation ledger.[53]

*The Registration Ledger.* This ledger was bound in notebook form. It was the special duty of one of the student-apprentices to record in it the code numbers and pledge advance figures, so that it could be checked against the cancellation ledger at a later date.

*The Cancellation Ledger.* This was also a type of notebook ledger. It contained all the pertinent information recorded on the pawn tickets returned when goods were redeemed, that is, the code numbers and the principal and interest figures. The former were taken from this ledger in order to cancel out same in the registration ledger, and the latter were taken to match the totals in the counterman's account books.

*Ledger of Articles to be Redeemed Later (liu-ch'ü pu) and the Added Interest Ledger (liu-li pu).* After the expiration of a pawned item's full pledge period, all pawnshops had the right to sell the item at auction. But if a borrower did not wish it to be sold, there was a means by which he could prevent such action. It involved a cash payment on the spot (at a figure well below the amount necessary to redeem), the recomputation of interest, and a three or six month extension of interest payment; this prodecure was know as *liu-ch'ü* ("retaining for redemption").[54] The two ledgers in question were employed to record the renegotiated terms, as well as pertinent information entered in other ledgers at the time of the original transaction.

*The Master Pawn Ledger (tang-tsung pu) and the Master Shelf Ledger (chia-tsung pu).* The master pawn ledger was used to record the total amounts advanced each day on pledged items. At the end of the month, it showed the gross sum paid out under that month's standard code element. At the end of the year, this ledger was instrumental in balancing the books, since it contained the annual gross cash outlay on pledges. It was also convenient for reviewing the year's business fluctuations and for comparing the gross volume of business with that of previous years.

Pawnshops were sometimes full of unredeemed, full-pledge-period articles that had yet to be renegotiated by means of the *liu-ch'ü* process or sold off at auction. These were all listed in the master shelf ledger, which included both items stored upstairs and those kept in jewelry container cabinets. Since this ledger was an important element in the pawnshop's annual inventory, it was regarded as similar to master inventory ledgers used in regular shops.

*The Ledger of Boxed Articles (ts'un-hsiang pu).* This ledger was a record of the charges (1 or 2 percent of monies advanced on pledge) made for boxing items with a pawn value of less than $5.00 at borrowers' request. This income did not accrue to the pawnshop but to its personnel. Ledger entries were therefore utilized to compute monthly shares which were paid out to all employees.[55]

General Ledgers

*The Journal.* General ledgers used in pawnshops were more elaborate than those found in other industries in China during the period 1875 to 1928. The journal, for example, was a master ledger which recorded every cash transaction--whether disbursement or receipt--taking place in a pawnshop for whatever reason.[56] As such, it was a conflation of all the other in-house ledgers and accounts. Each evening after business hours, its figures had to tally with the total cash on hand and the total cash outlay for the day. If there was an error, it was then possible to search immediately for the source--perhaps a failure to make an entry somewhere --and to correct it before the memory of the employee responsible had faded.

Pages in the journal were divided horizontally into two sections. In the upper section were entered the reasons for and the particulars concerning receipts and disbursements. In the lower section, money totals were recorded. For the sake of clarity in scanning the pages, the top half of the lower section was used to record money taken in, with the character *shou* ("received") printed on it. The bottom half was reserved for cash disbursed and was printed with the character *chih* ("paid out").

*The Share-Capital Ledger (ku-pen pu).* The share-capital ledger was kept to apprise owners of bonuses and dividends, which were declared annually. The ledger was especially important in the case of partnerships, where stock shares were not always held in equal blocks.

*The Individual Account Ledger (wang-lai pu).* Pawnshops kept detailed records of all outside financial dealings, such as the raising of initial operating capital and additional funds, bank deposits and withdrawals, and external accounts payable and receivable. Thus, an individual account ledger was maintained, in which each amount was listed by name.

The ledger's pages were divided horizontally into two sections, the upper section for receipts, the lower for disbursements. The interest on each account was recorded on the date it was paid; and monthly and annual summaries were made of the shop's net balance on such accounts. If money on hand exceeded money paid out, it was carried on the books as a liability (i.e., as money owed by the pawnshop). Conversely, if funds paid out were more than those taken in, they were carried as pawnshop assets (i.e., as funds owed to the pawnshop).

*The Exchange Rate Ledger (tui-huan pu).* Most of the Chinese pawnbroking industry in the early part of the twentieth century used the silver dollar as the standard monetary unit of account,[57] but different forms of coinage entered pawnshops in the course of business transactions. Due to rapid fluctuations in the market value of metals, it was necessary to enter the rates of exchange in all pawnshop ledgers and keep a master exchange-rate ledger, in which rates were transcribed on a daily basis. (This ledger's accounts were usually arranged by type of coin.) So vital were these exchange rates that in themselves they could sometimes spell the difference between profit and loss for a pawnshop.[58]

*In-House Expense Ledgers (k'ai-chih pu).* These ledgers were used to account for wages, food (including occasional employee banquets), and miscellaneous expenses. Great control was exercised over these operating costs because there was always the fear that they might get out of hand due to the large staff size of a pawnshop.

*The Monthly Master Statement (yüeh-tsung pu).* This statement represented a summary of all pawnshop accounts and was sent each month to every shareholder. The statement employed the so-called "four pillar method" (*szu-chu fa*), itemizing receipts, which included interest on both principal (i.e., advances made on pledges) and various bank deposits; expenditures (wages, etc.); deposits of cash and securities; and money owed to banks and other businesses.

*The Annual Master Statement (nien-chung tsung-chieh).* The annual master statement of a large *tien* or *tang* shop was a compilation of twelve monthly master statements. Following long-established pawnbroking tradition, it was transcribed on special red paper. At a ceremony held every January on the pawnshop premises, copies of this document were formally presented to the shareholders.59 This ceremonial presentation was commonly termed *k'an hung-chang* (literally "to read the red account"). It was at the meeting, too, that the manager delivered his annual report on the "state of the pawnshop" and respectfully called for suggestions from shareholders as to ways in which the business might be improved during the following year.


Wages, Dividends and Commissions


Between 1875 and 1928, when pawnshop employees' room and board was rather good compared to that enjoyed by employees in other industries, their wages were in contrast quite meager. In Wuhan during the 1920s, for example, pay for top business and managerial personnel was twenty or thirty dollars per month, while lower-ranked student-apprentices earned a mere forty or fifty cents.60

Other forms of income, however, accrued to pawnshop employees. For instance, when the business reported a profit, they shared a dividend with stockholders. The split always favored the latter: 60 to 40 percent was the rule, 70 to 30 percent common in certain areas, and 80 to 20 percent not unknown. No matter what the percentage cut was for employees, all of them theoretically received some of it. And two formulas were applied to compute the actual amounts: payment was either keyed to wage or else it was determined by such factors as rank, seniority, and the complexity of work performed.

Apart from the above, certain commissions and customer charges were passed on to the employees.

## The Boxing Charge

The monthly payment to employees of the boxing proceeds was divided into ten equal shares, three going to the outer posts, four to the inner posts and three to the middle posts and student-apprentices combined.

## Commissions on Unclaimed Items and Garments and the Wrapping Surcharge

At the spring and autumn sales of full-pledge-period articles, pawnshops charged wholesalers a 6 percent commission (based on the pledge value of all items sold in lots) and clothing stores 1 percent (based on the value of garments). A wrapping surcharge of 1 percent was added to all successful bids. The sums thus raised were apportioned among pawnshop personnel. Out of ten equal shares, two went to the outer posts, six to the inner posts, and two to the middle posts and student-apprentices together.

## The Distribution of Interest

Pawnshops collected interest monthly on pledge loans but allowed borrowers a five-day grace period. A month was therefore reckoned at thirty-five days for bookkeeping purposes. By the same token, two months were reckoned at thirty-six days. If on the thirty-sixth day a borrower had not paid the previous month's installment, the pawnshop immediately charged him an additional full month's interest and distributed a like amount among the employees as a bonus.

## Pawning and Redeeming Commissions

The pawning commission was calculated daily and equaled 1 percent of the money advanced on pledge, half a percent each going to the outer posts and inner posts. The redemption commission was computed at 3 percent of the money taken in, 2 percent being received by the outer posts and 1 percent by the inner posts. [61]

From the foregoing, it can be seen that wages of pawnshop employees in most cases amounted to less than their dividends and commissions, but that when the latter were figured in, their over-all incomes were far from meager, according to contemporary standards.

## Pawnshops and Labor Unions

Increasingly during the course of the Republic, industrial workers and shop assistants agitated for better working conditions and decent wages. Pawnshop industry personnel were no exception and organized widely to form unions.

It is instructive to consider a comprehensive set of demands that the Shanghai Pawnshop Industry Labor Union made on behalf of its membership to the Shanghai Pawnbrokers' Guild in the late 1920s. The contents shed light not only on the expectations of *tien* and *tang* shop employees, but, by inference, also on the actual quality of their lives. A summary of the main demands follows.

1. Monthly wages for the following personnel should be:[62,63]

|  | ($) |
|---|---|
| Manager | 20 |
| Persons in charge of wrapping/ valuables/ funds | 19 |
| Countermen | 18 |
| Middle posts | 17 |
| Head student-apprentice | 16 |
| Second student-apprentice | 15 |
| Third student-apprentice | 14 |
| Fourth student-apprentice | 13 |
| Fifth student-apprentice | 12 |
| Sixth student-apprentice | 10 |
| Seventh student-apprentice | 8 |
| Eighth student-apprentice | 6 |
| Night-watchmen and cooks | 10 |

Student-apprentices who are learning the business and have not yet completed one full year of service should receive $2 per month. In their second year, the wage should be increased to $4 per month. After more than two full years of service, student-apprentices should draw their full wage. Double salary should be paid all employees for the month of December.

2. Pawning, redeeming and code number commissions should be as follows:[64]

|  | (%) |
| --- | --- |
| Pawning | 2 |
| Redemption | 3 (on interest) |
| Code Number | 1 |

3. Bonuses and dividends should be shared equally between labor and capital, except for 6 percent in guaranteed interest to shareholders.

4. Doubling up jobs and skipping ranks should be forbidden.

5. Statutory vacations: all employees should receive three months' paid vacation per year. Deductions from pay during this time should be forbidden.

6. Business hours: the working day should not exceed ten hours.

7. Lump sum gratuities and death benefits: employees who have reached the retirement age of sixty and who have served a full twenty years should receive a lump sum gratuity of from $500 to $1,000.

If an employee dies on the job, the pawnshop should pay death benefits to his survivors according to the following schedule:

|  | ($) |
| --- | --- |
| Employed less than 10 years | 200 |
| Employed less than 20 years | 400 |
| Employed more than 20 years | 500 |

8. Food and provisions: thirty cents should be added to the cost of preparing each meal per table.[65] Each table should receive $10 per festival banquet.

It can be taken that wages and benefits in the trade generally fell below these demands.

## Taxation of Pawnshops

Pawnshop taxation began in the early Ch'ing dynasty during the third year of the K'ang-hsi reign (1664), when the Board of Revenue and Population decreed that pawnshops had to pay an annual duty of 5, 4, 3 or 2.5 taels, depending on their size. Thus, at the beginning, tax rates in the pawnbroking industry were low. Then, in the sixth year of the Yung-cheng Emperor (1728), pawnshop trade regulations were established, requiring persons who wished to engage in pawnbroking to first state their intentions to the county magistrate, who would then forward an application for a business permit to the provincial treasurer. Duty--or tax--was still paid by the year, but it now had to be reported in detail to the Central Government Board of Finance, via the various provincial treasurers. The result of this new policy was that government for the first time exercised some real control over pawnbroking.[66, 67] Subsequently, pawnshop merchants were compelled to contribute funds toward coastal defense and other military expenses in addition to their regular annual tax. To this end, they were made to take out a supplementary business certificate, which listed the amount of their contribution. (It was called, appropriately, *t'ieh-chüan*, "certificate levy.")

During the course of the Kuang-hsü reign (1895-1908), taxation methods underwent many changes, and the tax rate itself became much higher. In 1897, for instance, all pawnshops, regardless of size, paid a uniform annual tax of 50 taels.

In republican times, the Ministry of Finance always considered the pawnbroking industry as "big business," despite the fact that the number of pawnshops was a fraction of what it had been a century before (less than five thousand as opposed to twenty-five thousand). Taxation was keyed once again to pawnshop size, that is, to its initial capitalization, as had been the case during the K'ang-hsi reign. Business permit costs were figured on a sliding scale tied to the prosperity (or lack of it) of a given pawnshop location.[68] The business permit was subject to an "effective period of certification" and had to be regularly renewed. Ministry of Finance figures for the pawnbroking industry in 1913 reveal that the usual length for this period was five years.[69]

## Pawn Ticket Handwriting Style and Terminology

Old Man Chi wanted to talk of his faith in
the walls of Peiping and urge Mr. Chien
not to be over-anxious, but he did not

> fully understand what Mr. Chien was
> saying. Mr. Chien's words were like the
> ideographs on a pawn ticket which, though
> recognizable as words, were written in so
> different a way that if one tried to guess
> the meaning he could be embarrassed by be-
> ing given the wrong article.[70]

If pawnshop account ledgers were models of clarity, pawn
tickets were studies in the obscure. Indeed, the handwriting style
used on the tickets was a "form unto itself"; it took up where
"grass writing" (ts'ao-shu) left off. Characters were deliberately
altered and simplified, even replaced by homophonous words (pai-
tzu) and phrases from local dialects. These modifications together
produced not only a kind of shorthand, but also a pawn ticket il-
legible to borrowers and decipherable only by the pawnshop
personnel.

About one thousand characters were used in bookkeeping and
outside business activities, while those employed daily in pawning
transactions came to less than four hundred. The particular four
hundred characters used varied markedly from place to place;
since anchors and ploughs never crossed the counter of a prosperous urban tien or tang shop, the abbreviated character forms for
these rural items never evolved there.

The handwriting style peculiar to a given pawnshop was passed
on from senior personnel to the student-apprentices, who--as
part of their training when they had no special duties to perform--
traced out and copied the characters in current use.

A special terminology was applied to pawned items that in effect
downgraded their value as recorded on the pawn tickets. There
were two reasons for this: to decrease the amount of money advanced, and to lessen the liability for damage during storage.
Thus, a piece of gold jewelry was often prefixed "dull" and silver,
"tarnished." Garments were "in bad condition," "worm-eaten,"
rotten" or "threadbare," especially if they were valuable silks, furs
or pelts. And, in like manner, copperware, tinware and wooden
utensils were frequently described as "worthless."[71]

Figure 3 provides an illustration of pawn ticket handwriting
style and terminology: to the left, listings of items; to the right,
a selection of numbers.[72]

52

Fig. 3  Pawn Ticket Handwriting

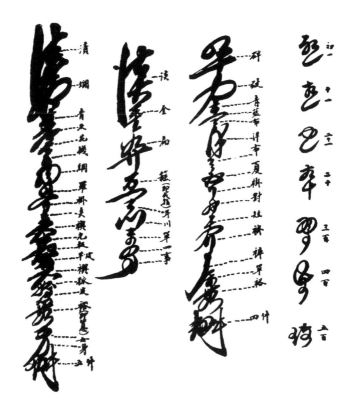

NOTES

## Part One

1. Abe Takeo 安部建夫 , "Shindai ni okeru tentōgyō no susei" 清代に於ける典當業の趨勢 [Pawnbroking Trends in the Ch'ing period], *Haneda hakushi shōju kinen tōyōshi ronsō* 9.8.3 (Tokyo, 1950): 1-36 (hereafter cited as Abe, *Pawnbroking*).

2. Miyazaki Michisaburō 宮崎道三郎 , *Miyazaki sensie hōseishi ronshū* 宮崎先生法制史論集 [Mr. Miyazaki's collected essays on the history of legal institutions] (Tokyo, 1929) (hereafter cited as Miyazaki, *Collected Essays*). His lecture on pawnshops, delivered in 1899, is on pp.11-14. For Taoist pawnbroking activities, see p. 8 below.

3. Tadao Miyashita, *The Currency and Financial System of Mainland China* (Seattle: University of Washington Press, 1966), p. 115.

4. Mi Kung-kan 宓公幹 , *Tien-tang lun* 典當論 [On Pawnbroking] (Shanghai: The Commercial Press Ltd., 1936), chap. 1.

5. Yang Chao-yü 楊肇遇 *Chung-kuo tien-tang yeh* 中國典當業 [The Chinese Pawnbroking Industry], Wan-yu wen-k'u series (Shanghai: The Commercial Press Ltd., 1929; reprint ed. Taipei: Hsüeh Hai Publishing House, 1972), chap. 1 (hereafter cired as Yang Chao-yü, *Chinese Pawnbroking*).

6. See *Erh-shih-wu shih* 二十五史 [Twenty-five dynastic histories], comp. K'ai Ming Book Company 1 (1934): 861 (p. 219 of the Hou Han Shu 後漢書 ).

7. Lien-sheng Yang, "Buddhist Monasteries and Four Money-Raising Institutions in Chinese History." *Harvard Journal of Asiatic Studies* 13 (1950): 174-191; see especially footnote, p. 179.

53

8. Conversations between Kenneth Chen and the writer in Los Angeles, March 1976.

9. Jacques Gernet, *Les aspects économiques du bouddhisme dans la société chinoise du Ve au Xe siècle* [Economic aspects of Buddhism in Chinese society from the fifth to the tenth centuries] (Saigon: Publications de L'École Française D'Extrême-Orient, 1956), p. 166, the text and note 3 (hereafter cited as Gernet, *Economic Aspects of Buddhism*).

10. See *Chan-kuo ts'e*, *Chao*, 6 戰國策趙卷第六, anno. Wu Shih-tao, vol. 5, p. 53 戰國策校註, 五.

11. "Pawn" as a noun in English also used to mean a person left as a hostage, as well as an earnest or pledge. Dryden wrote:

> He must leave behind, for pawns,
> His mother, wife, and son.

12. Miyazaki, *Collected Essays*.

13. For usury, see the *Kuan-tzu* 管子, XV 11-12, *Szu-pu ts'ung-k'an* 四部叢刊 edition, annotated by Fan Hsüan-ling (Shanghai: The Commercial Press Ltd,. 1929).

14. Lien-sheng Yang, *Money and Credit in China--A Short History*, Harvard-Yenching Institute Monographs, 12 (Cambridge, 1952), p. 5.

15. Ibid., p. 5.

16. Yang Chao-yü, *Chinese Pawnbroking*, chap. 1. He writes: "If it was money they wanted, they could not do without the pawnbroker; it was the pawnshop or nothing. There was no other road to cash. Hence the folk saying: 'Pawning is the poor man's back door.' One can see the intimacy between [the] poor man and the pawnbroker."

17. Since the impact of the pawnbroker in China was so widespread, one would think that a good deal would have been written about him, at least by economists. Such has not been the case. In Chinese poetry and literature, too, he seems to have been seen only "in the wings" and not as the subject of stage-center literary villainy.

There are many references to pawnshops in T'ang poetry as a source of ready cash for poets' drink, so many that pawning for wine was a cliché. But the Sung poet Ch'in Kuan--in a seven-character *chüeh-chü* sent to a finance minister describing his financial straits as a low-salaried government official newly moved to the capital--was at pains to explain that his daily pawning of spring clothes was not for drink but for food with which to ward off starvation. In the Ming *ch'uan-ch'i* drama *Ch'ing-shan chi* [The blue shirt], the "blue shirt" of the title was pawned by Po Chü-i and redeemed by the heroine, P'ei Hsing-nu.

Dealing with more recent times, the eponymous hero in Lu Hsün's *Ah-Q cheng-chuan* [The true story of Ah Q] pawns his quilt for two thousand cash. (As a youth, Lu Hsün made frequent trips to the pawnbroker to pay for his father's medical expenses.) In Pa Chin's novel *Chia* [Family], Fifth Uncle pawns his wife's jewelry to support a concubine. And in several novels of Lau Shaw, pawnbroking is mentioned (see p. 50 below).

Mao Tun, whose grandfather was a bookkeeper in a pawn-shop, makes a specific reference to pawnbroking in his short story *Lin-chia p'u-tzu* [The shop of the Lin family], written in 1932. The following passage illustrates the impact of Japanese aggression on the pawnbroker:

> Her [Mrs. Lin's] new silk dress had already gone to the only pawnshop in town to raise money for the maid's wages. An apprentice had taken it there at seven in the morning; it was after nine when he finally squeezed his way out of the crowd with two dollars in his hand. Afterwards, the pawnshop refused to do any more business that day. Two dollars! That was the highest price they would give for any article, no matter how much you had paid for it originally! This was called "two dollar ceiling." When a peasant, steeling himself against the cold, would peel off a cotton-padded jacket and hand it across the counter, the pawnshop clerk would raise it up, give it a shake, then fling it back with an angry "We don't want it!"
> (From *Spring Silkworms and Other Stories*, trans. Sidney Shapiro [Peking: Foreign Languages Press, 1956], p. 142.)

Finally, it should be noted that the phrase *shang-tang* ("to be swindled") and *shang-tang hsüeh-kuai* ("having been deceived, one learns caution") probably derive from the pawn-broker.

18. Paul Wheatley, *The Pivot of the Four Quarters* (Chicago: Aldine Publishing Company, 1971), p. 134.

19. From the Han dynasty on there were statutes regulating usury; but interest rate ceilings were all too often ignored by money-lenders, and prosecutions were very infrequent.

20. Kenneth Chen, *Buddhism in China* (Princeton: Princeton University Press, 1964), p. 264. Indeed, very early on, the balance of this exchange was tipped in favor of the temple treasuries.

21. Ibid., p. 401.

22. Miyazaki, *Collected Essays*, states that during the T'ang and Sung dynasties, Japanese Buddhist priests studying in China were to take the concept of the inexhaustible treasury back to Japanese temples.

23. The Chinese pawnshop seems to have been unique in this respect. The well-to-do often stored valuables there for a fee, the pawnshop acting as a kind of bank vault because of its size, construction, and comparatively fireproof nature.

24. Chen, *Buddhism in China*, p. 266. A shih is a dry measure for grain, a variable weight usually considered to be 133 1/3 pounds. As can be easily computed, interest accounted for some 27,000 pounds of grain.

25. Abe, *Pawnbroking*. He states that originally Buddhist temple pawnshops were set up "in aid of the poor." In this writer's opinion, Abe is implying that such pawnshops protected the needy from usury. If so, there is a parallel with the European *mont-de-piété* ("mount of piety"), a public pawnbroking establishment originating in Italy in the fifteenth century which loaned money at a low rate of interest to protect the poor from moneylenders.

26. Niida Noboru 仁井田陞, *Tōsō horitsu bunsho no kenkyū* 唐宋法律文書の研究 [A study of legal documents in the T'ang and Sung periods] (Tokyo: Cultural Institute, 1937), p. 229 (hereafter cited as Niida, *T'ang and Sung Legal Documents*).

27. Ibid., pp. 227 and 229. Concerning the p'i ("a piece of cloth"), Lien-sheng Yang, *Money and Credit*, p. 5, writes: "In the period of disunion following the fall of the Han empire until about 600, bolts of silk of a standard length and breadth were

used as the main medium of exchange. . . . This was also true
for the first part of the T'ang period (618-906). . . ." Inter-
estingly, the English word "pawn" comes from the Latin *pannus*,
a piece of cloth, which derives from the Greek πῆνος , a web,
and πήνη , a web or bobbin.

28. Niida, *T'ang and Sung Legal Documents*, p. 225.

29. Ibid., p. 229.

30. Chen, *Buddhism in China*, p. 266.

31. Lien-sheng Yang, "Buddhist Monasteries," p. 177.

32. *Kao-li tai* ("lending at high interest") is the general term for
    usury, and *hsi-hsüeh kuei* ("blook-sucking demon") the
    rather colorful modern vernacular term for usurer.

33. Kenneth Chen, "The Economic Background of the Hui-Ch'ang
    Suppression of Buddhism," *Harvard Journal of Asiatic Studies*
    19 (1956): 67-105; see especially p. 102.

34. Niida, *T'ang and Sung Legal Documents*, p. 229ff.

35. Pawnshop interest rates were at their highest during the
    T'ang-Sung period; 25 to 50 percent per month was not un-
    common, even though pawn loans in the T'ang dynasty could
    not by statute exceed 5 percent per month. Disregarding
    regional variations brought about by natural disaster or re-
    bellion, interest rates steadily declined over the centuries.
    By republican times 90 percent of all pawnshops charged
    between 2 percent and 4 percent per month. (See Lo Kuo-hsien
    and Chen Han-seng, "Pawnshop and Peasantry," *Agrarian
    China*, a report in the International Research Series of the
    Institute of Pacific Relations [Chicago: University of Chicago
    Press, 1938], pp. 188-93.)

36. Abe, *Pawnbroking*. The temple was usually accessible to
    peasants, both in terms of distance and reception. Niida ob-
    serves that it had always been easy for them to borrow from
    the temple pawnshop, and that even those who did have to
    travel a long way in order to pawn knew they would not be
    turned away. One can therefore speculate that once peasant
    borrowing--following seasonal rhythms--had become habitual,
    and a dependence on the temple pawnshop thus created, the
    imposition of interest on loans, and then even higher interest,
    could not and did not deter the peasant borrower. This
    pattern then quite naturally extended to the newer lay pawnshop.

37. Niida, *T'ang and Sung Legal Documents*, p. 229. If grain was borrowed, the pledge period generally extended to the next harvest, at which time the borrower could get a grace period of twenty days. However, if he then failed to repay (that is, defaulted on) the loan, he would be punished. (The Japanese text does not specify the punishment.)

38. Sogabe Shizuo 曾我部静雄 , "Sōdai no shichiya" 宋代の質屋 [Pawnshops in the Sung Period], *Shakai keizai shi-gaku* 社會經濟史學 21: 469-78.

39. Gernet, *Economic Aspects of Buddhism*, p. 170.

40. Lien-sheng Yang, *Money and Credit*, p. 71.

41. Hino Kaizaburō 日野開三郎 , "Sōdai chōseiko no hatten ni tsuite" 宋代長生庫の發展に就いて [Concerning the development of the *chōseiko* in the Sung dynasty], *Saga Ryukoku Gakkai Kiyō* 4 (1953), astracted in *Sōdai kenkyū bunken teiyō* 宋代研究文獻提要 [Abstracts of Japanese books and articles concerning the Sung] (Tokyo: Oriental Library, 1961), pp. 279-80.

42. Jacques Gernet, *La vie quotidienne en Chine à la veille de l'invasion mongole 1250-1276* [Daily life in China on the eve of the Mongol invasion, 1250-1276] (Paris: Librairie Hachette, 1959), pp. 73-75.

43. Miyazaki, *Collected Essays*.

44. See both Miyazaki, *Collected Essays* and Lien-sheng Yang, *Money and Credit*, p. 71.

45. Lien-sheng Yang, *Money and Credit*, p. 71.

46. Ibid., p. 6. The truth of Lien-sheng Yang's remark that most people forgot pawnbroking was once limited to temple precincts is borne out by Yang Chao-yü's book *Chung-kuo tien-tang yeh*. In his exhaustive coverage of pawnbroking in China, Yang Chao-yü never mentions Buddhism in connection with it.

47. Mark Elvin, *The Pattern of the Chinese Past* (Stanford University Press, 1973), p. 235.

48. Ibid., pp. 249-50, and p. 334, note 37.

49. Abe, *Pawnbroking*, p. 9.

50. Lien-sheng Yang, *Money and Credit*, p. 73.

51. Abe, *Pawnbroking*, p. 9. He argues that salt merchants and pawnbrokers had long been in competition, and that when the salt trade declined, it was natural for the former to "move in" on the latter.

52. This monthly payment figure of 3 percent was merely the tip of the iceberg; there was a host of additional charges borne by the borrower. (See Part Two.)

53. Abe, *Pawnbroking*, and Lien-sheng Yang, *Money and Credit*, p. 74 and p. 99.

54. Abe, *Pawnbroking*.

55. Lien-sheng Yang, *Money and Credit*, p. 71.

56. Abe, *Pawnbroking*, p. 9. See also Yang Chao-yü, *Chinese Pawnbroking*, chap. 2.

57. An 技 could be of Fukienese origin. Elvin, *Chinese Past*, writes that in the twelfth century, due to increasing population pressures on the land, many Fukienese emigrated south. Evidently resourceful and highly motivated, they did very well. A contemporary source said: "Nine out of ten pawnbrokers in Hua-chou (in Kwangtung) are Fukienese. The Fukienese resolutely put their empty hands to work, and those who come south over the mountains often become rich." See pp. 209-10, and p. 331, note 12.

58. Lien-sheng Yang, *Money and Credit*, p. 74.

59. Abe, *Pawnbroking*.

60. This is not to suggest that *chih* and *ya* shops had been unknown in the cities or *tien* and *tang* shops strangers to rural areas. On the contrary, the former had been common on the back streets and outskirts of cities, and the latter seen occasionally in market towns.

61. Lo and Chen, "Pawnshop and Peasantry."

62. As banking gained ground in late imperial times, the savings bank function of the pawnshops largely disappeared.

63. Two points should be made. The first is that the government in the nineteenth century also sometimes invested in *tang* shops, and *tien* shops were by no means completely underwritten by public funding. The second point is that the Shansi banks were able to charge the lowest rates of any of

the banks because "money from [the] government treasuries
was deposited with them either at a very low interest payment
or at none at all." By mid-century, Shansi banks held interest
rates in Peking to 0.4 or 0.5 percent, and to 0.6 percent in
Soochow, while the other banks, both traditional and modern,
held theirs between 0.7 and 1.2 percent during the same period.
See Lien-sheng Yang, *Money and Credit*, pp. 99–100.

64   Iseki Takao 井關孝雄, *Shina shomin kin'yū ron* 支那
庶民金融論 [A treatise on native financial organs among
the common people in China] (Tokyo: Gakugeisha, 1941), p. 77
(hereafter cited as Iseki, *Financial Organs in China*). The
large publicly funded *tien (kung-chi tien)* usually required a
capitalization of 500,000 yüan. The name *tien* remained (after
the withdrawal of public funds) and designated a large pawnshop of fixed capitalization, interest rates and tax schedule.

65.   Ibid., p. 91.

66.   Ibid., p. 91 ff.

67.   Lien-sheng Yang, *Money and Credit*, p. 72.

68.   Iseki, *Financial Organs in China*, p. 91.

69.   Lien-sheng Yang, *Money and Credit*, p. 72.

70.   Iseki, *Financial Organs in China*, p. 91.

71.   Ibid., p. 91. As evidence of this "expansion," Iseki refers to
the *Chi-tung* region (East Hopei), where in 1937 there were
thirty-three *tai-tang*, only three of which operated at a loss.

72.   See both Iseki, *Financial Organs in China*, p. 91 ff. and
Lien-sheng Yang, *Money and Credit*, p. 72.

73.   Lo and Chen, "Pawnshop and Peasantry."

74.   Ibid. The extremely low value of the average pawn ticket had
been noted as early as the 1890s. See T. R. Jernigan, *China's
Business Methods and Policy* (London: T. Fisher Unwin, 1904).
Jernigan was the American consul general in Shanghai in the
last days of the Ch'ing dynasty.

75.   Lo and Chen, "Pawnshop and Peasantry."

76.   R. H. Tawney, *Land and Labor in China* (1932; reprint ed.,
New York: Octagon Books, Inc., 1964) pp. 60–61.

77. Bizarre as this second reason sounds, it was a legitimate concern of the pawnbroker. Yang Chao-yü says in chapter 5 of *Chinese Pawnbroking*: "It is also possible to speak of some troublesome areas in the [pawnbroking] business. Of articles received in pledge, clothing now constitutes the greatest part. In recent years there has been a rapid turnaround in clothing styles and fashions. . . . What was stylish at the time of pawning will have been old-fashioned when the full pledge period is reached. Consequently the value of garments falls. This loss of capital is grounds for possible anxiety on the part of the pawnbroker."

78. Conversations between Chou Hung-hsiang and the writer in Los Angeles, August 1976.

79. Hayashi Kohei 林耕平, "Chū-shi kakuchi ni okeru tentōgyō 中支各地に於ける典當業 [The pawnshop business in various parts of Central China], *Mantetsu chōsa geppō* 23.3 (March 1943): 69-101; 23.4 (April 1943): 43-89.

80. Tadao Miyashita, *Currency and Financial System*, p. 115.

81. Cheng Cho-yüan, *Monetary Affairs of Communist China* (Hong Kong: Union Research Institute, 1955), p. 139.

82. Katherine Huang Hsiao, *Money and Monetary Policy in Communist China* (New York and London: Columbia University Press, 1971), p. 61. Quite apart from state sources for loans, W. J. F. Jenner, who spent two years in Peking in the early 1960s, as well as more recent visitors to that city, reports the existence of state commission shops, through which persons can raise cash. Such shops undertake to resell secondhand articles left in their care. A nominal fee is charged for this service.

83. Rick Johnson, "Swindlers or Saviours—China's Pawnshops," *Echo* (1974): 42-46. The municipal department in charge of pawnshops in its jurisdiction, whether running them outright, or controlling their activity if they were privately owned, was (and presumably still is) the Bureau of Finance. As a case in point, it was this bureau in Taipei's municipal government that put a 10 percent interest ceiling on the city's private pawnshops in the late 1950s, and which later limited such shops to one per ten thousand inhabitants. Thus, in 1974 there were 174.

84. It is not clear from the sources whether in fact municipally run pawnshops differ in appearance from privately owned ones.

85. For an exhaustive description of the former mainland Chinese pawnshop, see Part Two below. This and the following brief remarks are included merely for purposes of comparison.

Part Two

1. C. F. Gordon Cumming, *Wanderings in China* (Edinburgh and London: William Blackwood & Sons, 1888), pp. 25-26. The sentence "Some foreigners thus dispose of their furs in the winter season" is no doubt a slip of the pen and should read either ". . . furs *after* the winter season" or ". . . furs in the *spring* season."

   Mrs. Cumming's account is surprisingly accurate both as regards pawnshop description and procedure, and pawning patterns. The rate of interest, "ranging from 20 to 36 per cent," is for the complete pledge period, not a monthly figure. This writer has come upon no reference in any language to rooftop weaponry, such as Mrs. Cumming graphically details. However, pawnshops were prime targets of rebel attack. It was usual, when a town was sacked, for the yamen to be smashed up first, the jail broken open and prisoners released, and then for the pawnshops to be looted. (See Susan Naquin, *Millenarian Rebellion in China: The Eight Trigrams Uprising of 1813* [New Haven: Yale University Press, 1976], pp. 140-42, 224, 226-27.)

2. In point of fact, throughout Kwangtung (and thus in the city of Canton), a *tang* was the smallest pawnshop, while a *ya* was the largest (and the *tien* shop unknown). This order is the reverse of that found in all other provinces of China, where the ranking was *tien, tang, chih* and *ya*--in terms of (a) highest capitalization to lowest, (b) lowest interest rate to highest, (c) longest redemption period to shortest, and (d) most tax paid to least. Whereas Mrs. Cumming was actually referring to a *ya*-type pawnshop when she used the phrase "first-class pawn-tower," in the rest of China it would be taken to mean a *tien* or *tang* shop.

3. There is of course Lien-sheng Yang's masterly synthesis on the pawnshop in his *Money and Credit in China*, pp. 71-75, noted above. But by its nature, Yang's section on pawnbroking precludes elaboration and detail.

4. Fire was an ever-present danger because almost all contiguous structures were built of wood.

5. The reason for this is that Kwangtung pawnshops did not have
to pay a business license fee, but did have to pay a revenue
tax. Hence the *hsiang* character.

6. Strangers to Peking often mistook these pawnshops for money
changers or banks. Lien-sheng Yang, *Money and Credit*,
p. 72, remarks that *all* Peking pawnshops exhibited "two
strings of imitation cash of large size" and omitted the "*tang*"
character entirely. This would appear to be too categorical.
Madame Li Kuei-fen and Mr. Cheng Tung, both natives of
Peking and currently residing in Los Angeles, attest to the fact
that "*tang*" was used with some frequency as a pawnshop sign
instead of strings of cash, or in addition to them (conversations
with this writer, 1975).

7. The well-to-do invariably sent their servants to make transactions for them.

8. Courtesy of Mr. Cheng Tung. It was common for pawnshops
located in the middle of a block to front onto two streets, and
thus to have two main entrances, opposite each other across
the foyer.

9. It is possible that counters were high also for psychological
reasons; pawnshop personnel loomed large, and borrowers were
placed in a subservient position.

10. None of the available sources offers a reason for this difference.

11. See the section on organization below (pp. 25-31) for more
information on this post.

12. In more recent times, steel was sometimes used in shelf
construction.

13. Overvalued or bogus items were sold at special sales. In the
period under discussion, the practice of passing off fakes was
a common one, as was that of pawning stolen property. Against
the latter there were elaborate safeguards. For these reasons
and a variety of others, pawnbrokers usually tried to under-
value pledges.

14. According to Yang Chao-yü, many *ya* shops were run by ban-
dits, by deserters from the military, and by common criminals
(what might be termed *éléments déclassés*), as distinct from
"honest *tang* shop merchants."

15. Sometimes the "radius" was a mere fifty households.

16. If the Kiangsu Province Pawnshop Regulations of 1913 and 1927 (see the section on business below) can be taken to be indicative of the rest of China, then pawnbrokers did not have to indemnify in cases of damage or destruction caused by war, theft, vandalism, fire or *force majeure.* Be that as it may, pawnbrokers were still responsible for loss resulting from carelessness or accident on the part of the staff, and no longer wished to bear this heavy financial burden. Clearly the drift was toward limited partnership and thus limited liability.

17. During the 1920s, shares of pawnshop stock were issued with more frequency in the foreign concessions than elsewhere, in imitation of the organization of limited liability companies there.

18. This type of contract was called a *ho-t'ung.* There seems to have been some leeway as to the form it took, each partnership more or less deciding for itself. But it does appear that, once executed, the contractual terms were faithfully adhered to.

19. By statute, a pawnbroker with insufficient capital had to discontinue operation until such time as he could raise additional capital. See the section on business below.

20. There is a discrepancy here between Iseki, *Financial Organs in China,* p. 77, and Yang Chao-yü, *Chinese Pawnbroking,* chap. 3, over the filing of the "*tien* certificate." It will be recalled that in Part One above, *kung-tien* and *kung-tang* shops were "not considered to be set up for private profit," this being a legacy from the days of government funding, even though--in terms of the period under discussion--it was an incorrect assumption. *Szu-chih, szu-ya,* and *szu-an* (in Fukien and Kwangtung), on the other hand, as their names suggest, were privately operated. This writer cited Iseki, *Financial Organs in China* (see also note 64 above) as the authority for these assertations. Yang Chao-yü, however, believes that *kung-tien* and *kung-tang* referred to those pawnshops that had filed a "*tien* certificate" and had therefore reported themselves "publicly," whereas *szu-chih, szu-ya,* and *szu-an* referred to those pawnshops that had not reported themselves and operated "privately," that is to say, illegally.

21. Not only was the structure complex, it was also quite rigid; and employees tended to be promoted very slowly (much more slowly in fact than in other shops or businesses). Advancement was in terms of time in grade and seniority, and skipping over jobs up the organizational ladder was forbidden. It was not uncommon for an employee to be still among the ranks of the student-apprentices after ten years' work. (Mr. Cheng Tung reports that lower-level student-apprentices were nothing

more than the "body servants" of key business and managerial personnel.)

22. Because of the nature of his duties, the public relations officer was a local man who was well connected in his (and the pawnshop's) community.

23. A head counterman was sometimes known as a *ch'ao-feng*. The term dates from the Han dynasty and referred to a wealthy person who occasionally attended the Emperor's morning court audience. (In much later times it was also used colloquially for a shop proprietor or manager.) But although a head counterman was called a *ch'ao-feng*, there appears to have been a difference between him and a *ch'ao-feng* per se. The latter was an adviser, almost a referee. When a head counterman received an item and was unable to determine its value or authenticity, he passed it on to a *ch'ao-feng* for advice. Over the centuries, this distinction was lost. (As late as the 1920s, a head counterman was always called a *ch'ao-feng* in Anhui.)

24. The selling of unredeemed pledges at auction dates from the Six Dynasties, when pawnshops were restricted to Buddhist temple precincts. (For auction sales in Buddhist monasteries, see Chen, *Buddhism in China,* p. 265, and Lien-sheng Yang, "Buddhist Monasteries," pp. 174-91.) Yang Chao-yü is incorrect when he asserts (in *Chinese Pawnbroking,* chap. 5): "Selling items which had come to full term [and which had not been redeemed] was not within the original scope of pawnbroking, but rather was a result of the nature of the business, as it developed."

25. This is a case of the velvet glove and the mailed fist. Countermen who did not possess a good business sense were considered unfit to perform the duties of their job.

26. Sometimes the two posts of "wrapping" and "valuables" were both filled by one person. This depended on the size of a pawnshop's business.

27. Here again, the posts of "funds" and "bookkeeping" were sometimes combined. But Yang Chao-yü wryly remarks (chap. 3) that "because the Chinese customarily put heavy emphasis on human nature and light emphasis on regulations, and also wished to avoid corruption, it [seemed] prudent to divide the [two] duties."

28. A single transaction often comprised several items in one "lot." The question of redeeming some items from a "lot" and renegotiating terms for the remainder will be taken up later.

29. In some cases there were two writers in pawnshops, one making the pawn ledger entry, the other simultaneously writing out the pawn ticket.

30. The *ch'i-feng* was a special seal used to match up documents and prevent fraud. The procedure was as follows: the edges of the documents in question--for example, two identical copies of a contract--were aligned or allowed to overlap slightly. Then the seal was affixed in such a manner that half its image appeared on each document. This insured a tally at a later date and made forgery virtually impossible, which is not to suggest that it was never attempted. *Ch'i-feng* literally means "to bestride a seam."

31. In very large pawnshops, two groups of men were involved, some shops having four or five packagers.

32. In Wuhan tri-city area pawnshops, packaging and labeling were done by one man. In Shanghai, however, two men (or groups of men) were engaged in this work.

33. "Boxing" was different from regular packaging. See p. 41, above.

34. This was a harsh provision. It can only be assumed that its object was to force a poor borrower not to default, and thus not leave the pawnshop with an item of very low resale value on its hands.

35. Article Nine of the 1913 regulations provided that items from single lots could be redeemed. If this was done, the lot had to be reevaluated and a new pawn ticket issued. Substitute items could not be used as pledges to bring the initial lot back "up to strength," so to speak.

36. This custom applied mainly to personal debts and obligations. But just as everyone "wound up his affairs" at this time, so did business also balance its accounts. Pawnbroking, however, was unique. The pawning transaction was not personal, but impersonal, and it was certainly not necessary for the borrower and the lender to know one another. Thus, the year-end settlement did not prevail in the pawnshop. The vast majority of pledge periods extended beyond the first of January or expired before then, and it was borrowing anew from the pawnbroker at the end of the year which, to a great extent and especially among the poor, allowed the custom of New Year settlement to endure.

37. For further information on the correlation between agriculture and pawning, see Lo and Chen, "Pawnshop and Peasantry."

38. This "swarming" phenomenon was more pronounced in the countryside than in the cities. Year-round pawnbroking business fluctuations were noticeably milder in the treaty ports, where industry and commerce proceeded more or less on an even keel, irrespective of season.

39. This quotation is from the *Chin-men tsa-chi*, ed. Chang T'ao, reprinted in Yang Chao-yü, *Chinese Pawnbroking*, chap. 1.

40. During peaceful conditions under the Manchus, two or three year terms were average. In republican times, pledges for as short a period as ten months were known.

41. Fluctuations in interest as a result of civil unrest or natural disaster were usually self-correcting after normalcy returned.

42. Yang Chao-yü, *Chinese Pawnbroking*, chap. 1. Their true motive was presumably that they were competing to cash in on the year-end custom of settling all unpaid debts.

43. Street violence in Shanghai in the late 1920s caused pawnshops there to close at midnight on New Year's Eve rather than remain open until dawn as had been customary.

44. Another cost was that of valuable shelf space.

45. During inflationary periods, of course, all expenses went up, taxes included. In republican times, some pawnshops also fell prey to warlords and found themselves forced to contribute to the support of troop levies.

46. None of the other sources sheds any light on this provision.

47. Even by current western standards, this seems a long time indeed. Mr. Cheng Tung comments, however, that pawnshop personnel worked under great pressure, often in sweatshop conditions, and might well have used the two-month holiday to regain their health. (Conversations with the writer, 1975.)

48. This seal contained the three characters *mou-yüeh ch'ü*, that is, "redeemed during month X."

49. This is the first mention of such a ledger. See the following section, under "Master Shelf Ledger."

50. Fraudulent sale of pawn tickets or their circulation on the outside could severely damage a pawnshop's business.

51. The names of pawnshops almost always contained two characters, whose import was usually one of tender inducement,

especially to the poor. References to *Kuan-yin* ("mercy") and "good fortune" were common.

52. This sentence, which limits a pawnshop's liability, is somewhat at variance with number twelve of the Kiangsu regulations of 1927 (see page 33 above).

53. Although the Chinese pawnbroking industry during the period under review had not adopted the latest in western accounting methods, its level of bookkeeping was nevertheless very high when compared to that of contemporary businesses and shops in China.

54. The amount of added interest here hinged on the total amount of the money advanced on pledge and how much original interest--if any--had been paid in. When recomputing, the borrower could decide whether he wished to carry the payments over three or six months, and the pawnshop was obliged to comply.

55. In theory, all shares were equal. In practice, senior business and managerial personnel received more of this special income than did other employees.

56. All transactions were entered here in chronological order almost as they occurred, that is, essentially at the same time as their entry in appropriate ledgers throughout the pawnshop.

57. The silver ounce (*liang*) preceded the silver dollar as the standard unit in pawnbroking.

58. This was because pawnshop interest rate ceilings were pegged, as already described.

59. In Peking, this event occurred on the first of January.

60. The figures for Shanghai in the same period were lower.

61. The existence of these commissions would seem to have tested the loyalty of countermen to their employers in the extreme. For they alone were the judges of pawn value.

62. The inner post of "Bookkeeping" is not listed.

63. The position of "Eighth Student-Apprentice" does not appear on the pawnshop organizational chart on p. 27 above.

64. A code number commission would seem to be a completely new demand on the part of the union.

65. Chou Hung-hsiang estimates that eight to ten employees sat at each table.

66. For example, under these regulations, pawnshops that failed did not have to pay tax from the date of failure, provided they surrendered their business permits.

67. Before republican times, there was no term in Chinese for "business taxation," whereas *tang-shui* ("pawnshop tax") and *ya-shui* ("brokerage license tax") were in use during the Ch'ing dynasty. When the taxation of regular businesses became common under republican rule, both the pawnshop tax and the brokerage license tax (like the wine and tobacco license tax) were placed under the general category of "business tax."

68. Some permit costs were linked to business profit rather than location. (It can be argued, however, that this amounted to the same thing. A pawnshop in a prosperous location was bound to make a larger profit than one in an out-of-the-way rural area.)

69. Ministry of Finance figures for 1913 are from *A Financial History of the Republic of China*, ed. Chia Shih-i, reprinted in Yang Chao-yü, *Chinese Pawnbroking*, chap. 10. The effective period of certification was ten years in Kiangsu and Chekiang, twenty years in Shensi, and thirty years in Kansu. In Kwantung, on the other hand, it was only one year.

70. Lau Shaw 老舍 , *Szu-shih t'ung-t'ang* 四世同堂 [Four generations under one roof]. The quotation is from *The Yellow Storm*, condensed and translated by Ida Pruit (London: Victor Gollancz Ltd., 1951), p. 25.

71. There were regional variations in ordinary and legitimate descriptions of pawned articles. In Hankow, for example, the color of garments was recorded on pawn tickets. In Shanghai, it was not.

72. Yang Chao-yü, *Chinese Pawnbroking* (chap. 8), reports a shift in the 1920s to a more legible "cursive style" (*hsing-shu*) in the writing of pawn tickets, but how widespread this practice was is not known. Also, in recent years, the date of transaction, previously written on pawn tickets, was affixed with a wooden seal. Both illustrations are from *Chinese Pawnbroking* (also chap. 8).

# GLOSSARY

| | | | |
|---|---|---|---|
| *Ah-Q cheng chuan* 阿Q正傳 | *The True Story of Ah Q* | | 55 |
| an 按 | pawnshop | | 10 |
| Chang Chih-tung 張之洞 | | | 35 |
| ch'ang-sheng ch'ien 長生錢 | long life cash | | 5 |
| ch'ang-sheng k'u 長生庫 | long life treasury, | | 5 |
| | long life treasury funds, | | 5 |
| | temple pawnshop (Sung), | | 8 |
| | pawnshop (literary expression) | | 8 |
| ch'ao-feng 朝奉 | head counterman | | 65 |
| chi-fu p'u 寄附鋪 | lay pawnshop (T'ang) | | 8 |
| Chi-tung ti-ch'ü 冀東地區 | Chi-tung region (East Hopei) | | 60 |
| ch'i-cheng 契證 | a contract | | 7 |
| ch'i-feng 騎縫 | to bestride [a] seam | | 30 |
| *Chia* 家 | *Family* | | 55 |
| chia-tsung pu 架總簿 | master shelf ledger | | 44 |
| chiao-chih 交質 | to exchange political hostages | | 3 |
| chieh-k'u 解庫 | lay pawnshop (Sung) | | 8 |
| chieh-tien k'u 解典庫 | lay pawnshop (Yüan) | | 9 |
| Ch'ien-lung 乾隆 | | | 9 |
| *Ch'ien-tzu wen* 千字文 | *The Thousand Character Classic* | | 42 |

| chih | 支 | paid out | 45 |
|---|---|---|---|
| chih | 質 | hostage, | 3 |
| | | a pledge, | 3 |
| | | [temple] pawnshop, | 3 |
| | | pawnshop | 10 |
| chih-ch'ien | 質錢 | pawning money | 3 |
| chih-chü | 質舉 | pawn loans | 3 |
| chih-k'u | 質庫 | temple pawnshop (Six Dynasties and T'ang), | 3 |
| | | lay pawnshop (Sung) | 8 |
| Chin-men tsa-chi | 津門雜記 | A Tientsin Miscellany | 67 |
| Ch'in Kuan | 秦觀 | | 54 |
| ching-li | 經理 | pawnshop manager | 26 |
| ch'ing-p'iao che | 清票者 | person in charge of the clearing and checking of pawn tickets | 40 |
| Ch'ing-shan chi | 青衫記 | The Blue Shirt | 55 |
| ch'ing-shui liu-yüeh | 清水六月 | the unmuddied waters of the sixth moon (the slack sixth month) | 34 |
| chu-lien pi-ho | 珠聯璧合 | matching pearls and jades ('matching exactly') | 43 |
| ch'u-na | 出納 | receipts and expenditures | 26 |
| ch'uan-ch'i | 傳奇 | drama (Ming) | 55 |
| chung-ch'üeh | 中缺 | middle posts | 26 |
| chü | 局 | pawning partnership | 8 |
| ch'ü-yin | 取印 | a seal signifying redemption | 40 |
| chüan-ch'i | 券契 | a contract | 7 |
| chüeh-chü | 絕句 | stanza of four lines | 54 |
| erh-kuei | 二櫃 | second counterman | 26 |

| | | |
|---|---|---|
| fa-shang sheng-hsi 發商生息 | entrusting to merchants to produce profit | 10 |
| fang-shou jen 防守人 | guarantor | 7 |
| ho-t'ung 合同 | a contract | 64 |
| hsi-hsüeh kuei 吸血鬼 | usurer | 57 |
| hsia-chia 下架 | to remove unredeemed goods from the shelves | 36 |
| hsia-tsao 下灶 | lower cook | 31 |
| hsiang 餉 | revenue (literally, 'provisions' or 'funds to buy provisions') | 63 |
| hsiang-an 餉按 | pawnshop (Kwangtung) | 21 |
| hsiang-ya 餉押 | pawnshop (Kwangtung) | 21 |
| hsieh-yeh tien-tien 歇業典店 | closed down pawnshop | 12 |
| hsing-shu 行書 | cursive writing style | 69 |
| hsüeh-sheng 學生 | student-apprentices | 26 |
| Hu-kuang 湖廣 | provinces of Hunan and Hupeh | 35 |
| Hui-Ch'ang 會昌 | | 7 |
| Huo Hsin-yüeh 霍昕悦 | | 6 |
| ju-lou 入樓 | 'Put Upstairs' | 40 |
| ju-shih 入飾 | 'Put in Jewelry Box' | 40 |
| k'ai-chih pu 開支簿 | in-house expense ledgers | 46 |
| k'an hung-chang 看紅帳 | to read the red account | 46 |
| K'ang-hsi 康熙 | | 10 |
| kao-li tai 高利貸 | usury | 57 |
| keng-fu 更夫 | night watchman | 31 |
| ku-chia kung-cheng 估價公正 | fair appraisals | 15 |

74

| | | | |
|---|---|---|---|
| ku-pen pu | 股本簿 | share-capital ledger | 45 |
| ku-tung | 股東 | shareholders | 26 |
| kua-erh | 掛二 | 20% markup on a 'lot' of unredeemed goods | 37 |
| kua-hao pu | 掛號簿 | registration ledger | 40 |
| kua-i | 掛一 | 10% markup on a 'lot' of unredeemed goods | 37 |
| k'uai-chi | 會計 | accounting | 26 |
| kuan-chang | 管帳 | accountant | 29 |
| kuan-ch'ien | 管錢 | person in charge of funds | 29 |
| kuan-li yüan | 管理員 | managerial personnel | 29 |
| kuan-lou | 管樓 | upstairs manager | 29 |
| kuan-pao | 管包 | person in charge of wrapping | 29 |
| kuan-shih | 管事 | pawnshop manager | 26 |
| kuan-shih | 管飾 | person in charge of valuables | 29 |
| Kuang-hsü | 光緒 | | 9 |
| k'uei-hao | 虧號 | unredeemed goods of poor quality marked down at sales ("a loss 'lot'") | 37 |
| kung-chi tien | 公濟典 | publicly-funded pawnshop | 11 |
| kung-i | 公益 | public welfare | 5 |
| kung-tang | 公當 | *tang* pawnshop | 12 |
| kung-tien | 公典 | *tien* pawnshop | 12 |
| *Li-hsüeh chih-nan* | 吏學指南 | *Civil Servants' Manual* | 6 |
| liang | 兩 | ounce of silver | 68 |
| *Lin-chia p'u-tzu* | 林家舖子 | *The Shop of the Lin Family* | 55 |

| | | |
|---|---|---|
| liu-ch'ü 留取 | retaining for redemption | 44 |
| liu-ch'ü pu 留取簿 | ledger of articles kept to be redeemed at a later date | 44 |
| liu-li pu 留利簿 | the added interest ledger | 44 |
| liu-shui pu 流水簿 | the journal | 39 |
| mou-yüeh ch'ü 某月取 | redeemed during month X | 67 |
| Mu-pang kuei-t'iao 木榜規條 | 'Regulations Posted on Wooden Signboards' | 31 |
| nei-ch'üeh 內缺 | inner posts | 26 |
| nien-chung tsung-chieh 年終總結 | annual master statement | 46 |
| pai-tsu 白字 | homophonous words | 51 |
| pao-cheng 保證 | special guarantee | 7 |
| pao-kuan 保管 | safekeeping of valuables | 26 |
| pao-kuan an-ch'üan 保管安全 | valuables stored in safety | 15 |
| p'i 疋 | piece of cloth | 6 |
| pu-p'iao 補票 | replacing the pawn ticket | 41 |
| san-kuei 三櫃 | third counterman | 26 |
| shang-tang 上當 | to be swindled | 55 |
| shang-tang hsüeh kuai 上當學乖 | having been deceived, one learns caution | 55 |
| shang-tsao 上灶 | upper cook | 31 |
| shichiya 質屋 | pawnshop (Japanese) | 3 |
| shih 石 | dry measure for grain | 56 |
| shou 收 | received | 45 |
| shou-kuei 首櫃 | head counterman | 26 |
| shou-shu liao 手數料 | handling fee | 12 |

| | | | |
|---|---|---|---|
| shui-mai | 稅買 | property tax | 8 |
| szu-an | 私按 | *an* pawnshop | 12 |
| szu-chih | 私質 | *chih* pawnshop | 12 |
| szu-chu fa | 四柱法 | four pillar method | 46 |
| szu-kuei | 四櫃 | fourth counterman | 26 |
| szu-ya | 私押 | *ya* pawnshop | 12 |
| ta-tang | 打當 | to sell unredeemed articles | 36 |
| tai-pu | 代步 | pawnbroking agency | 12 |
| tai-tang | 代當 | pawnbroking agency | 12 |
| tang | 當 | pawnshop | 11 |
| tang-pen | 當本 | money advanced on pledge | 42 |
| tang-p'iao | 當票 | pawn ticket | 40 |
| tang-pu | 當簿 | pawn ledger | 39 |
| tang-p'u | 當鋪 | pawnshop | 3 |
| tang-shui | 當稅 | pawnshop tax | 69 |
| tang-tsung pu | 當總簿 | master pawn ledger | 44 |
| ti-tang k'u | 抵當庫 | government-operated pawnshop | 8 |
| t'ieh-chüan | 帖捐 | certificate levy | 50 |
| tien | 典 | to mortgage,<br>collateral,<br>pawnshop | 6<br>6<br>7 |
| tien-chang | 典賬 | pawn ledger | 43 |
| tien-tang | 典當 | to pawn,<br>the giving of tribute,<br>pawnshop | 2<br>2<br>9 |
| tien-t'ieh | 典帖 | tien certificate | 25 |
| ting-fu | 丁賦 | poll-tax | 9 |

| | | |
|---|---|---|
| ts'ao-hsiao pu 草銷簿 | cancellation ledger | 40 |
| ts'ao-pu 草簿 | counterman's ledger | 39 |
| ts'ao-shu 草書 | grass (running-hand) writing style | 51 |
| ts'un-hsiang 存箱 | boxing | 41 |
| ts'un-hsiang pu 存箱簿 | ledger of boxed articles | 44 |
| tu-tieh 度牒 | ordination license for a Buddhist or Taoist priest | 8 |
| tui-huan pu 兌換簿 | exchange rate ledger | 45 |
| tui-t'ung 對同 | matched and agreed to | 40 |
| t'un-tang 囤當 | pawn hoarding | 11 |
| tzu-ch'ien chia 子錢家 | interest-making specialists | 4 |
| tzu-hao 字號 | a goods 'lot' | 36 |
| tz'u-t'ang yin 祠堂銀 | ancestral temple silver | 5 |
| wai-ch'üeh 外缺 | outer posts | 26 |
| wai-hsi 外席 | public relations officer | 26 |
| Wang 王 | (a common surname) | 43 |
| wang-lai pu 往來簿 | individual account ledger | 45 |
| wen-shu 文書 | documents | 5 |
| wu-chin ts'ai 無盡財 | inexhaustible resources | 5 |
| wu-chin tsang 無盡藏 | inexhaustible treasury | 2 |
| Wu-tsung 武宗 | | 7 |
| ya 押 | pawnshop | 10 |
| ya-shui 牙稅 | brokerage license tax | 69 |
| yeh-kuei 業規 | trade regulations | 31 |

78

ying-yeh 營業      business      26

ying-yeh yüan 營業員      business personnel      26

Yung-cheng 雍正      50

yüeh-tsung pu 月總簿      monthly master statement      46

# BIBLIOGRAPHY

Abe Takeo. "Shindai ni okeru tentōgyō no susei" [Pawnbroking Trends in the Ch'ing period]. *Haneda hakushi shōju kinen tōyōshi ronsō* 9.8.3 (1950): 1-36.

Chen, Kenneth. *Buddhism in China.* Princeton: Princeton University Press, 1964.

_____. "The Economic Background of the Hui-Ch'ang Suppression of Buddhism." *Harvard Journal of Asiatic Studies* 19 (1956): 67-105.

Cheng Cho-yuan. *Monetary Affairs of Communist China.* Hong Kong: Union Research Institute, 1955.

Elvin, Mark. *The Pattern of the Chinese Past.* Stanford: Stanford University Press, 1973.

Gernet, Jacques. *Les aspects économiques du bouddhisme dans la société chinoise du Ve au Xe siècle.* Saigon: Publications de L'École Français D'Extrême-Orient 39 (1956).

_____. *La vie quotidienne en Chine à la veille de l'invasion mongole 1250-1276.* Paris: Librairie Hachette, 1959.

Hayashi Kōhei. "Chū-shi kakuchi okeru tentōgyō" [The pawnshop business in various parts of Central China]. *Mantetsu chōsa geppō* 23 (March 1943): 69-101; 23 (April 1943): 43-89.

Hino Kaizaburō. "Sōdai chōseiko no hatten ni tsuite" [Concerning the development of the chōseiko in the Sung dynasty]. *Saga Ryukoku Gakkai Kiyō* 4 (1953). Abstracted in *Sōdai kenkyū bunken teiyō* [Abstracts of Japanese books and articles concerning the Sung], Tokyo: Oriental Library, 1961, pp. 279-80.

Hsiao, Katherine Huang. *Money and Monetary Policy in Communist China.* New York and London: Columbia University Press, 1971.

Iseki Takao. *Shina shomin kin'yū ron* [A treatise on native financial organs among the common people in China]. Tokyo: Gakugeisha, 1941.

Jernigan, T. R. *China's Business Methods and Policy.* London: T. Fisher Unwin, 1904.

Johnston, Rick. "Swindlers or Saviours--China's Pawnshops." *Echo* (1974): 42-46. (Published in English in Taiwan.)

King, Frank H. H. *Money and Monetary Policy in China.* Cambridge: Harvard University Press, 1965.

Lo Kuo-hsien and Chen Han-seng. "Pawnshop and Peasantry." In *Agrarian China,* a report in the International Research Series of the Institute of Pacific Relations, pp. 188-93. Chicago: University of Chicago Press, 1938.

McElderry, Andrea Lee. *Shanghai Old-Style Banks (Ch'ien-chuang), 1800-1935.* Michigan Papers in Chinese Studies, no. 25. Ann Arbor: University of Michigan Center for Chinese Studies, 1976.

Mi Kung-kan. *Tien-tang lun* [On pawnbroking]. Shanghai: The Commercial Press, Ltd., 1936.

Miyashita Tadao. *The Currency and Financial System of Mainland China.* Seattle: University of Washington Press, 1966.

Miyazaki Michisaburō. *Miyazaki sensei hōseishi ronshū* [Mr. Miyazaki's collected essays on the history of legal institutions]. Tokyo, 1929.

Niida Noboru. *Tōsō horitsu bunsho no kenkyū* [A study of legal documents in the T'ang and Sung periods]. Tokyo: Cultural Institute, 1937.

Sogabe Shizuo. "Sōdai no shichiya" [Pawnshops in the Sung period]. *Shakai keizai shigaku* 21: 469-78.

Swann, Nancy Lee. *Food and Money in Ancient China.* Princeton: Princeton University Press, 1950.

Wheatley, Paul. *The Pivot of the Four Quarters.* Chicago: Aldine Publishing Company, 1971.

Yang Chao-yü. *Chung-kuo tien-tang yeh* [The Chinese Pawnbroking industry]. Wan-yu wen-k'u series. Shanghai: The Commercial Press, Ltd., 1929. Reprint ed., Taipei: Hsüeh Hai Publishing House, 1972.

Yang Lien-sheng. "Buddhist Monasteries and Four Money-Raising Institutions in Chinese History." *Harvard Journal of Asiatic Studies* 13 (1950): 174-91.

_____. *Money and Credit in China--A Short History*. Harvard-Yenching Institute Monographs, no. 12. Cambridge: Harvard University Press, 1952.

## MICHIGAN PAPERS IN CHINESE STUDIES

No. 2. *The Cultural Revolution: 1967 in Review*, four essays by Michel Oksenberg, Carl Riskin, Robert Scalapino, and Ezra Vogel.

No. 3. *Two Studies in Chinese Literature*, by Li Chi and Dale Johnson.

No. 4. *Early Communist China: Two Studies*, by Ronald Suleski and Daniel Bays.

No. 5. *The Chinese Economy, ca. 1870-1911*, by Albert Feuerwerker.

No. 8. *Two Twelfth Century Texts on Chinese Painting*, by Robert J. Maeda.

No. 9. *The Economy of Communist China, 1949-1969*, by Chu-yuan Cheng.

No. 10. *Educated Youth and the Cultural Revolution in China*, by Martin Singer.

No. 11. *Premodern China: A Bibliographical Introduction*, by Chun-shu Chang.

No. 12. *Two Studies on Ming History*, by Charles O. Hucker.

No. 13. *Nineteenth Century China: Five Imperialist Perspectives*, selected by Dilip Basu, edited by Rhoads Murphey.

No. 14. *Modern China, 1840-1972: An Introduction to Sources and Research Aids*, by Andrew J. Nathan.

No. 15. *Women in China: Studies in Social Change and Feminism*, edited by Marilyn B. Young.

No. 17. *China's Allocation of Fixed Capital Investment, 1952-1957*, by Chu-yuan Cheng.

No. 18. *Health, Conflict, and the Chinese Political System*, by David M. Lampton.

No. 19. *Chinese and Japanese Music-Dramas*, edited by J. I. Crump and William P. Malm.

No. 21. *Rebellion in Nineteenth-Century China*, by Albert Feuerwerker.

No. 22. *Between Two Plenums: China's Intraleadership Conflict, 1959-1962*, by Ellis Joffe.

No. 23. *"Proletarian Hegemony" in the Chinese Revolution and the Canton Commune of 1927*, by S. Bernard Thomas.

No. 24. *Chinese Communist Materials at the Bureau of Investigation Archives, Taiwan*, by Peter Donovan, Carl. E. Dorris, and Lawrence R. Sullivan.

No. 25. *Shanghai Old-Style Banks (Ch'ien-chuang), 1800-1935*, by Andrea Lee McElderry.

No. 26. *The Sian Incident: A Pivotal Point in Modern Chinese History*, by Tien-wei Wu.

No. 27. *State and Society in Eighteenth-Century China: The Ch'ing Empire in Its Glory*, by Albert Feuerwerker.

No. 28. *Intellectual Ferment for Political Reforms in Taiwan, 1971-1973*, by Mab Huang.

No. 29. *The Foreign Establishment in China in the Early Twentieth Century*, by Albert Feuerwerker.

No. 31. *Economic Trends in the Republic of China, 1912-1949*, by Albert Feuerwerker.

No. 32. *Chang Ch'un-ch'iao and Shanghai's January Revolution*, by Andrew G. Walder.

No. 33. *Central Documents and Politburo Politics in China*, by Kenneth Lieberthal.

No. 34. *The Ming Dynasty: Its Origins and Evolving Institutions*, by Charles O. Hucker.

No. 35. *Double Jeopardy: A Critique of Seven Yüan Courtroom Dramas*, by Ching-Hsi Perng.

No. 36. *Chinese Domestic Politics and Foreign Policy in the 1970s*, by Allen S. Whiting.

No. 37. *Shanghai, 1925: Urban Nationalism and the Defense of Foreign Privilege*, by Nicholas R. Clifford.

## MICHIGAN ABSTRACTS OF CHINESE AND
## JAPANESE WORKS ON CHINESE HISTORY

No. 1. *The Ming Tribute Grain System*, by Hoshi Ayao, translated by Mark Elvin.

No. 2. *Commerce and Society in Sung China*, by Shiba Yoshinobu, translated by Mark Elvin.

No. 3. *Transport in Transition: The Evolution of Traditional Shipping in China*, translations by Andrew Watson.

No. 4. *Japanese Perspectives on China's Early Modernization: A Bibliographical Survey*, by K. H. Kim.

No. 5. *The Silk Industry in Ch'ing China*, by Shih Min-hsiung, translated by E-tu Zen Sun.

No. 6. *The Pawnshop in China*, by T. S. Whelan.

## NONSERIES PUBLICATION

*Index to the "Chan-kuo Ts'e,"* by Sharon Fidler and J. I. Crump. A companion volume to the *Chan-kuo Ts'e*, translated by J. I. Crump (Oxford: Clarendon Press, 1970).

Michigan Papers and Abstracts available from:

Center for Chinese Studies
The University of Michigan
Lane Hall (Publications)
Ann Arbor, Mi 48109 USA

Prepaid Orders Only
write for complete price listing